Visual Factfinder

STARS

AND

PLANETS

Visual Factfinder

STARS
AND
PLANETS

JAMES MUIRDEN

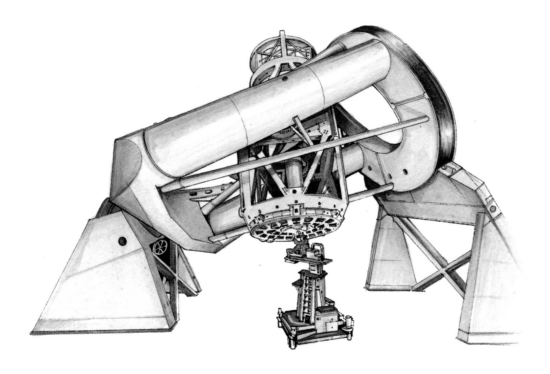

Kingfisher Books

NEW YORK

KINGFISHER BOOKS
Grisewood & Dempsey Inc.
95 Madison Avenue
New York, New York 10016

First American edition 1993
2 4 6 8 10 9 7 5 3 1 (lib. bdg.)
2 4 6 8 10 9 7 5 3 1 (pbk.)
Copyright © Grisewood & Dempsey 1993

Library of Congress Cataloging-in-Publication Data
Muirden, James.
Stars and planets / James Muirden.—1st American ed.
p.   cm.—(Visual factfinder)
Includes index.
Summary: Text and illustrations, diagrams, tables, and charts
present information on such astronomical topics as our solar system,
galaxies, black holes, and space exploration.
1. Astronomy—Juvenile literature. [1. Astronomy.] I. Title.
II. Series.
QB48.M949   1993
520—dc20   93-20104   CIP   AC

ISBN 1-85697-852-4 (lib. bdg.)
ISBN 1-85697-851-6 (pbk.)

Printed in Spain

Series Editor: Michèle Byam
Editor: Cynthia O'Neill
Series Designer: Ralph Pitchford
Design Assistant: Sandra Begnor
Picture Research: Su Alexander, Elaine Willis

Additional help from Stuart Atkinson, Shaun Barlow,
Nicky Barber, Andy Archer, Janet Woronkowicz, Hilary Bird

CONTENTS

About this Factfinder

Through the dynamic combination of words and pictures, this encyclopedic reference book presents a wealth of facts and figures in an instantly accessible form. It examines the infinite universe of which our Earth is such a tiny part, and traces the development of astronomy and space exploration.

Up-to-date photographs reveal the scenery of space, and provide a further source of visual information on areas such as space technology and the planets.

Captions give in-depth information on subjects such as the planets and their satellites, the stars and galaxies, the fate of the universe, and the exploration of space.

Short text essays introduce each of the main areas of astronomy and space travel, including a close look at each planet and strange space objects such as black holes.

Venus

Through a telescope Venus appears as a gleaming, silvery gem. But appearances deceive, because the planet is in fact a rocky waste, hotter than Mercury and spread out under a choking carbon dioxide atmosphere that is denser than water. Sulfuric acid droplets fall on the surface from clouds that permanently cast an orange gloom. The surface features shown on these pages (mountains, craters, and volcanoes) were detected by spacecraft radar —the only way of probing the thick clouds.

▲ Although the surface conditions are totally different, Venus is almost a twin of the Earth in size. Venus is very hot because its thick atmosphere is very efficient at holding in the Sun's heat. (Distances not to scale.)

► The orbit of Venus lies between the Earth and the Sun. This means it can be seen only in the twilight after sunset or before sunrise. Venus is sometimes called the morning star or the evening star.

Earth

Venus

▼ Venus's atmosphere is made up almost entirely of carbon dioxide, produced in vast amounts from erupting volcanoes when the planet was young. Sunlight penetrates the atmosphere and warms the surface of the planet. The ground radiates heat waves, but they cannot escape back into space because of the thick cloud layer. The heat is trapped, warming the planet still more.

▲ The surface of Venus is completely hidden by dense clouds.

miles above the surface

80% of Sun's light is reflected by cloud layer

Some heat escapes

Upper cloud layer

Middle cloud layer

Lower cloud layer

Sunlight

Thick clouds trap most heat from the surface

VENUS DATAFILE

STRUCTURE

Atmosphere
Crust
Mantle

Partly-molten metallic core

Diameter: 7,545 mi.
Mass: 0.82 × Earth
Density: 5.2 (water = 1)
Minimum distance from Sun: 67 million mi.
Maximum distance from Sun: 68 million mi.
Minimum distance from Earth: 25 million mi.
Day/night: 117 Earth days
Length of year: 225 Earth days
Tilt of axis: 12° 42'
Surface gravity: 0.90 × Earth
Temperature: 900°F average
Satellites: 0

VENUS

◄ An artist's impression of Venus's surface, based on radar information. The highland areas, or continents, are colored yellow. The mountain Maxwell Montes is 7 mi. (12 km) high. Its peaks are the second highest in the Solar System. About 80 percent of the surface of Venus is covered with dusty, rocky lava plains, which have smothered most of the early craters. A well-known crater, Cleopatra, is 100 mi. (160 km) across.

ISHTAR TERRA
(highland area, as large as Australia)
Cleopatra
Maxwell Montes
SEDNA PLANITIA
LEDA PLANITIA
Theia Mons
Sif Gula Mons
APHRODITE TERRA
(highland area, as large as Africa)
LAVINIA PLANITIA

► The Magellan spacecraft mapped 99 percent of the surface of Venus in 1990–1992. It recorded features as small in size as a football field.

◄ Maat Mons is a volcanic feature on Venus, 5 mi. (8 km) high. Radar information from Magellan was processed by computer technology to produce this image.

► Sulfur dioxide from early volcanic activity has helped to form dense sulfuric acid clouds. These spread in a corrosive mist over the surface of Venus.

22

Maps present the geography of space, revealing where the Solar System lies in the Milky Way, and showing the constellations of the northern and southern night skies.

BEYOND THE SOLAR SYSTEM
The Milky Way

The Sun is just one of a hundred billion stars, existing in space in a vast "star-city." This city is our galaxy, which we call the Milky Way. The softly-shining band of light in our night sky is also called the Milky Way, and is the edge-on view of our own galaxy. The Milky Way is spiral in shape, and the Sun is found out toward its "edge." The galaxy is so huge that it would take a beam of light about 100,000 years to cross from one edge to the other, even though light travels at almost 186,000 mi. (300,000 km) a second. Huge areas of the Milky Way are unexplored because our view of them is so poor—it is like trying to see people at the other side of a crowd. Dark clouds block the light from the center of the galaxy, increasing the astronomers' problems. However, observing other galaxies has helped to build up a picture of what our own is like.

THE MILKY WAY
The Milky Way is a barred spiral galaxy, with two arms that rotate slowly. The area in which our Sun is found takes about 225 million years to go around once. At the center is a bright halo of old stars that formed with the galaxy, 14 billion years ago. The arms contain vast nebulae of gas and dust where new stars are being born.

HOW A GALAXY BEGINS
Galaxies began as huge masses of dark gas. As they shrink under the pressure of gravity (1), the gas at the center becomes dense enough to start forming stars. The galaxies start turning (2), and if it is fast enough it flings out the outer areas into a flat disk, forming a spiral (3) or barred galaxy. Galaxies that turn slowly or not at all become spherical or elliptical in shape.

▲ A slowly-spinning mass of gas starts to collapse, and the first stars are formed at the center. As the cloud shrinks, its turning speed increases.

▲ Gas clouds meet in the swirling disk, and attract more clouds because of their extra gravity. Stars start to form here too.

▲ There is no gas left at the center to make new stars, but the arms are rich in raw star material. The galaxy is now in its prime of life.

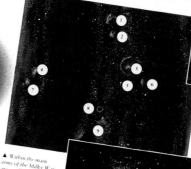

▲ Within the main arms of the Milky Way are smaller arms where stars and nebulae are more closely connected. This illustration shows some of the Sun's neighbors in the galaxy.

1 Cone Nebula
2 Rosette Nebula
3 Orion Nebula
4 Lagoon Nebula
5 Solar System
6 California Nebula
7 Trifid Nebula
8 Vela Supernova Remnant
9 N. American Nebula

◄ This panorama of our galaxy was obtained by combining several photographs taken of the Milky Way from different parts of the world. If you imagine the right and left ends joined together, with your head inside the ring, this is how the Milky Way would appear to someone floating in space.

▼ The Orion Nebula is about 30 light-years across and 1,600 light-years away. It was once dark, but millions of years ago stars began forming inside it, and their radiation makes the nebula glow.

▲ The Milky Way is rich in dark nebulae. However, the galaxy is foggy with tiny particles that act as a color filter. The effect causes objects like this nebula to appear red to us on Earth.

MILKY WAY DATAFILE

Diameter:
130,000 light-years
Thickness of spiral arms:
3,000 light-years (approx.)
Thickness of central bulge:
10,000 light-years
Diameter of central bulge:
20,000 light-years
Total mass: 110 billion × Sun
Average density (estimate):
0.0000000000000000000°
(water = 1)
Age: 14 billion years
Time to rotate once:
(Position of Sun)
225 million years
Distance of Sun from center:
30,000 light-years
Satellite galaxies: 2

47

Detailed artwork illustrates the diversity of planets and moons other than our own, as well as portraying the life and (sometimes explosive) death of a star.

Schematic diagrams help to explain the mysteries of the universe in easy stages — the formation of galaxies and how scientists think everything began and may end.

Quick-reference datafiles provide essential statistics on the planets, making it easy to compare them, and also supply at-a-glance facts about the Milky Way, our galaxy.

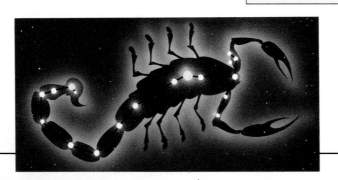

The greatest achievement in the history of space exploration has been landing astronauts on the Moon.

STARS
AND
PLANETS

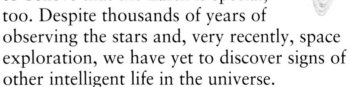

Centuries ago, early civilizations looked to the skies and thought that the Earth must be the center of the universe, with the Sun and stars in orbit around it. As our understanding of the universe grew, human beings began to realize how small and unimportant the Earth is. It is just one small planet whirling around an ordinary star, in a galaxy of at least 100 billion stars. But we are right to believe that the Earth is special, too. Despite thousands of years of observing the stars and, very recently, space exploration, we have yet to discover signs of other intelligent life in the universe.

Stars and Planets provides an illustrated guide to our knowledge of space. Topics covered range from the Sun and the planets, to theories on the beginning of the universe. The life and death of stars is explained, and astronomical achievements through history are listed. There is still a great deal we do not know about the universe. The final section highlights the space technology that has made distant planets familiar to us, and that may help us to learn more about space in the future.

James Muirden

COSMIC TIME

A Timescale of the Universe

The universe is everything that exists. All the planets, stars, and the "star cities," or galaxies, are part of the universe, and so is all of space. The universe has no center, or edge—it seems to go on for ever. Most astronomers believe that the universe began about 15 billion years ago, in a huge explosion they call the Big Bang. They think that during the Big Bang the raw material of everything found in the universe was created in an instant of time, far shorter than anything we can measure or imagine. There is evidence to support this idea, because the galaxies in the universe seem to be flying apart, as if from an explosion. Scientists have also detected the faint heat-waves left over from a vast explosion. Since time began with the Big Bang, we cannot ask what caused the explosion, as nothing can exist without time. The Big Bang is the ultimate mystery.

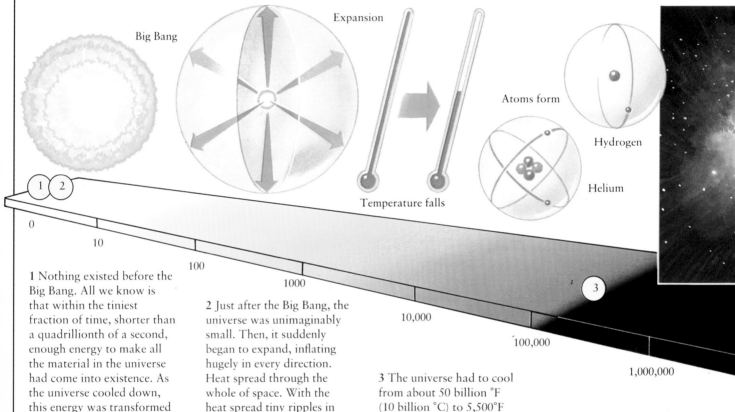

Big Bang

Expansion

Atoms form

Hydrogen

Helium

Temperature falls

0
10
100
1000
10,000
100,000
1,000,000

1 Nothing existed before the Big Bang. All we know is that within the tiniest fraction of time, shorter than a quadrillionth of a second, enough energy to make all the material in the universe had come into existence. As the universe cooled down, this energy was transformed into atomic particles.

2 Just after the Big Bang, the universe was unimaginably small. Then, it suddenly began to expand, inflating hugely in every direction. Heat spread through the whole of space. With the heat spread tiny ripples in the radiation given out by the explosion.

3 The universe had to cool from about 50 billion °F (10 billion °C) to 5,500°F (3,000°C) before atoms could form. Atoms are the minute units of matter. The atoms were mainly hydrogen, which is the simplest and most plentiful substance found in the universe. The rest were more complex atoms of helium.

4 Hydrogen and helium filled the universe with a thin, dark fog. The gas atoms in denser parts of the fog were pulled into separate, much smaller clouds by gravity. (Gravity is the force by which objects attract one another.) The centers of the clouds, where the gas atoms were packed together, heated up, giving birth to stars as the galaxies formed.

FACTS ABOUT MATTER AND ENERGY

- Matter, or mass, is all the material in the universe. The famous scientist Albert Einstein (1879–1955) suggested that energy can be turned into matter, and that matter can be turned into energy. His theory is the basis for all our ideas on the beginning of the universe.
- Radiation is a form of energy. Particles with high-energy are a form of radiation. Some radiation, like that from a fire, can be felt as heat.

◄ *Astronomers can examine the past and see what the universe was like long before the Earth formed. Light travels at great speed— 186,000 mi./s (300,000 km/s). However, distances in space are so huge that light still takes years to reach us from the nearest stars—the ones that shine in the night sky. Light takes billions of years to reach us from remote galaxies. The light we receive from a distant galaxy now shows that galaxy, not as it is today, but as it used to be all that time ago. This means astronomers can observe objects formed when the universe was young.*

▼ *In 1992, it was announced that the* Cosmic Background Explorer *satellite (COBE) had traced the background radiation and "ripples" left over from the Big Bang, 15 billion years before.*

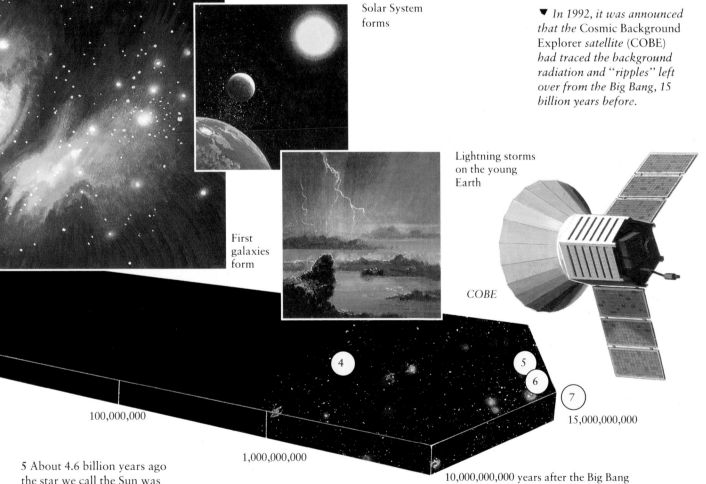

Solar System forms

First galaxies form

Lightning storms on the young Earth

COBE

4

5

6

7

100,000,000

1,000,000,000

15,000,000,000

10,000,000,000 years after the Big Bang

5 About 4.6 billion years ago the star we call the Sun was formed. Around it was a cloud of gas and dust containing substances such as carbon and oxygen. These had been formed in older stars and blasted out into space when the stars died. These substances came together to form the planets.

6 The first living cells appeared on Earth 3.5 billion years ago. How life began is uncertain. Maybe lightning storms provided the energy to start chemical reactions in the "soup" of elements on the young planet.

7 It has taken one ten-thousandth of the time since the Big Bang for recognizable humans to develop from apes. Today, scientists try to work out the story of the universe by sending into space satellites which look back across time.

THE SOLAR SYSTEM

Beginnings

We live on a small rocky planet we call the Earth, which travels through space on an orbit, or path, around a star we call the Sun. The Earth is part of the Solar System—the name we give to the Sun and the family of planets, asteroids, and comets that orbit it. This family reaches far into space—the Solar System is about a million times wider than Earth. "Solar" means "of the Sun," and the Sun is by far the most important member of the family. It is about 740 times more massive than all the planets put together. Because of its great size, it has a powerful gravitational pull, and this pull keeps the Solar System together and controls the movements of the planets. The Solar System began about 4.6 billion years ago, when a cloud of hydrogen, helium, and a tiny percentage of other elements started to condense into a cluster of stars. One of these stars was the Sun.

THE BIRTH OF THE SOLAR SYSTEM

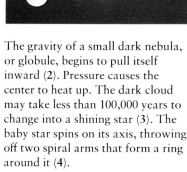

The "empty" space between stars in fact contains hydrogen atoms and tiny grains of solid material. The grains lie very far apart from each other. However, in some regions of a galaxy the grains are found much closer together, forming dark clouds of gas and dust. These regions are called nebulae.

Stars are formed from a nebula when the material in the nebula is given a shake, making it break up into much smaller nebulae (1). For example, a star might explode nearby and send out powerful energy waves. In some colliding galaxies, stars are formed where nebulae meet and pass through each other.

The gravity of a small dark nebula, or globule, begins to pull itself inward (2). Pressure causes the center to heat up. The dark cloud may take less than 100,000 years to change into a shining star (3). The baby star spins on its axis, throwing off two spiral arms that form a ring around it (4).

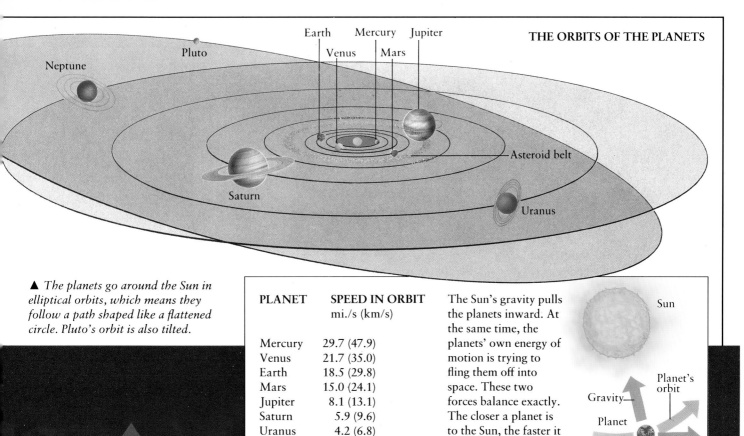

▲ *The planets go around the Sun in elliptical orbits, which means they follow a path shaped like a flattened circle. Pluto's orbit is also tilted.*

PLANET	SPEED IN ORBIT mi./s (km/s)
Mercury	29.7 (47.9)
Venus	21.7 (35.0)
Earth	18.5 (29.8)
Mars	15.0 (24.1)
Jupiter	8.1 (13.1)
Saturn	5.9 (9.6)
Uranus	4.2 (6.8)
Neptune	3.3 (5.4)
Pluto	2.9 (4.7)

The Sun's gravity pulls the planets inward. At the same time, the planets' own energy of motion is trying to fling them off into space. These two forces balance exactly. The closer a planet is to the Sun, the faster it has to move to maintain this balance.

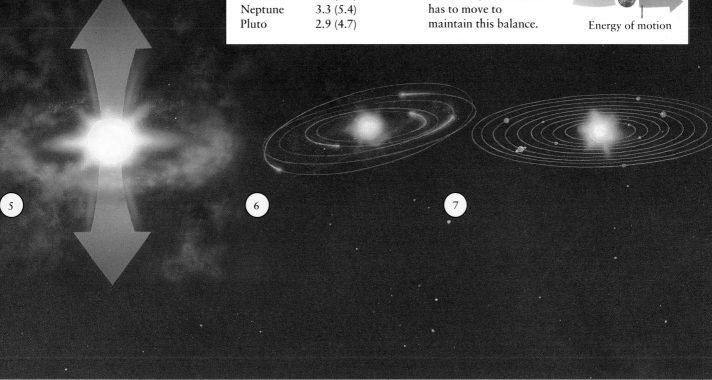

As a star like the Sun forms, the force of its inward collapse heats its center. When the temperature inside the star reaches millions of degrees, nuclear reactions are able to start. These send a new wave of energy outward (5), which keeps the star from shrinking further and blasts the remains of the nebula out into space.

The ring of gas and dust thrown out by our young Sun began to collect into fragments and solid grains of matter. Once these "planetesimals" reached a certain size, their gravity began to pull in other, smaller fragments, and they grew rapidly (6). Gradually they turned into the planets we know today (7).

The inner planets have hard surfaces. The giant outer planets grew into rocky globes too, but they then attracted the hydrogen and helium gases and icy particles that collected in the cold regions of the Solar System. Some smaller planetesimals became asteroids (*see pages 42–43*); others became moons of the planets.

13

The Sun

The Sun lies at the center of our Solar System, a fiercely-hot ball of gas nearly 900,000 mi. (1.4 million km) wide. Its appearance changes all the time: prominences leap from the Sun into space, and dark spots appear on its surface. Since its birth, some 4.6 billion years ago, the Sun has been the power station for the Earth and the other planets, providing them with their light and heat. The source of the Sun's energy lies deep inside its center, where the nuclear reactions that keep it shining take place.

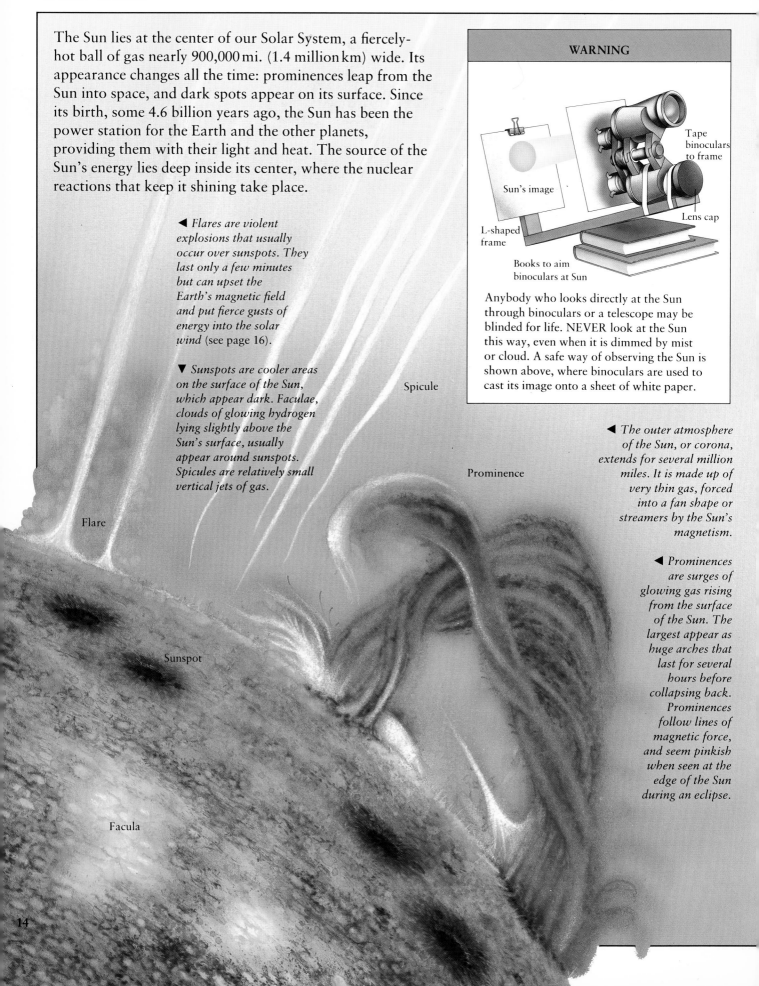

Tape binoculars to frame

Sun's image

L-shaped frame

Lens cap

Books to aim binoculars at Sun

◀ *Flares are violent explosions that usually occur over sunspots. They last only a few minutes but can upset the Earth's magnetic field and put fierce gusts of energy into the solar wind (see page 16).*

▼ *Sunspots are cooler areas on the surface of the Sun, which appear dark. Faculae, clouds of glowing hydrogen lying slightly above the Sun's surface, usually appear around sunspots. Spicules are relatively small vertical jets of gas.*

Spicule

Prominence

Flare

◀ *The outer atmosphere of the Sun, or corona, extends for several million miles. It is made up of very thin gas, forced into a fan shape or streamers by the Sun's magnetism.*

◀ *Prominences are surges of glowing gas rising from the surface of the Sun. The largest appear as huge arches that last for several hours before collapsing back. Prominences follow lines of magnetic force, and seem pinkish when seen at the edge of the Sun during an eclipse.*

Sunspot

Facula

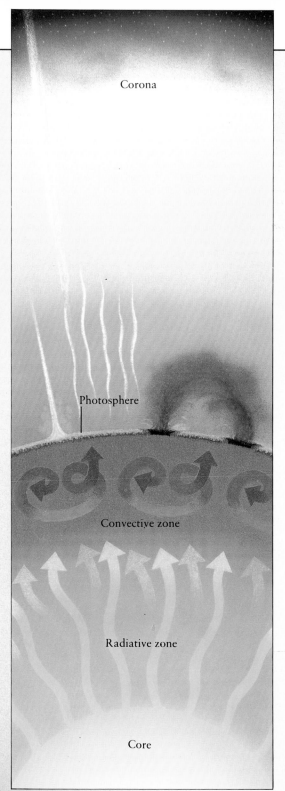

Corona

Photosphere

Convective zone

Radiative zone

Core

HOW THE SUN SHINES

The temperature at the center of the Sun is about 27 million °F (15 million °C). Here, the atoms that make up its main gas, hydrogen, have so much energy that they break apart, coming together again as helium gas. During this reaction, a burst of energy is given out. This energy drives the Sun. It is thought the Sun contains enough hydrogen to keep giving out energy for billions of years. As it uses up its fuel, our star will change (below).

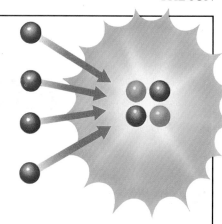

▶ *The Sun will continue to shine almost unchanged for several billion years. Meanwhile, the Earth will continue to pass through ice ages and warm periods as its orbit goes through a regular cycle of slight change.*

◀ *In about 5 billion years' time, energy from the Sun's huge core will make its outer layers expand. As our star swells and grows hotter, the water on Earth will start to boil away. Life forms will suffocate in the great heat.*

▶ *As the Sun turns into a red giant star, Earth will be scorched to a cinder, and its atmosphere will be stripped away. A few million years later the thin outer layers of the Sun will have consumed the Earth; Mars will probably escape.*

THE STRUCTURE OF THE SUN

Light and heat are produced in the core of the Sun. This energy then flows in waves through the radiative zone, with sufficient force to stop the vast bulk of the Sun from collapsing inward under gravity. The energy waves are weakened by this journey so that when they reach the convective zone they can radiate no further. Instead, the energy waves reach the visible surface of the Sun (the photosphere) by a violent churning motion called convection.

◀ *After the red giant stage, lasting about 100 million years, the Sun will run out of nuclear fuel. It will shrink and become a white dwarf star. From the surface of Mars (left) it will be a dim pinpoint. The Earth will no longer exist.*

15

Every second, the Sun loses 7 million tons of material, but all the material lost so far only amounts to less than 0.01 percent of its mass since it started shining. Of this amount, 4 million tons are turned into energy when protons and neutrons fuse together, giving out radiation and falling into the core. The Sun's lifetime is not limited by the amount of its fuel, but by the growth of its core. When the core reaches a certain size, the Sun will expand and it will start to destroy the Earth *(see page 15)*.

AN ECLIPSE OF THE SUN

Sun

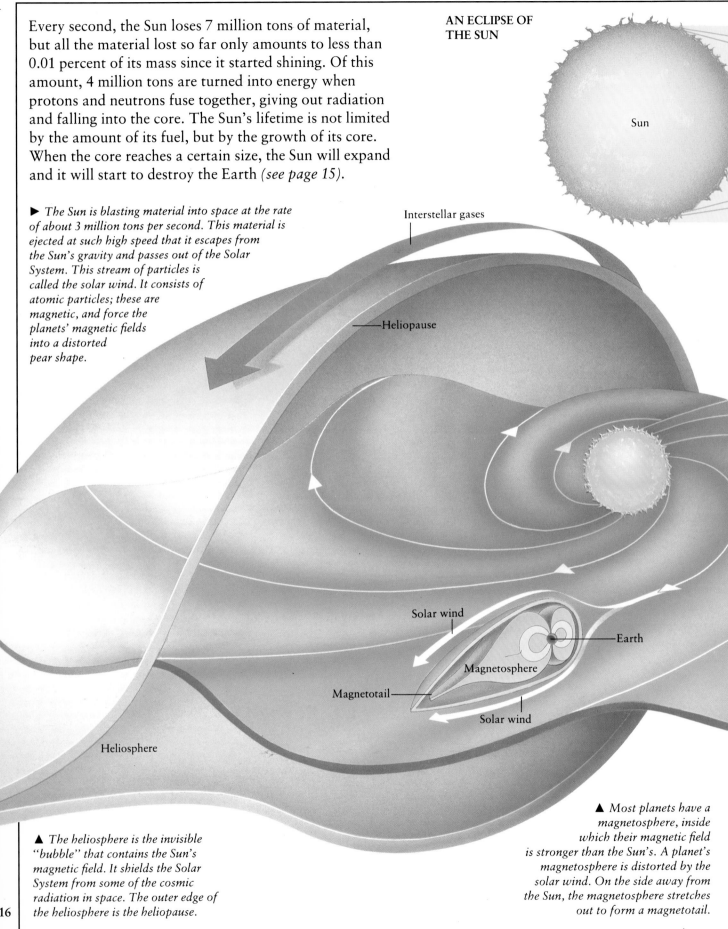

► *The Sun is blasting material into space at the rate of about 3 million tons per second. This material is ejected at such high speed that it escapes from the Sun's gravity and passes out of the Solar System. This stream of particles is called the solar wind. It consists of atomic particles; these are magnetic, and force the planets' magnetic fields into a distorted pear shape.*

Interstellar gases

Heliopause

Solar wind

Earth

Magnetosphere

Magnetotail

Solar wind

Heliosphere

▲ *The heliosphere is the invisible "bubble" that contains the Sun's magnetic field. It shields the Solar System from some of the cosmic radiation in space. The outer edge of the heliosphere is the heliopause.*

▲ *Most planets have a magnetosphere, inside which their magnetic field is stronger than the Sun's. A planet's magnetosphere is distorted by the solar wind. On the side away from the Sun, the magnetosphere stretches out to form a magnetotail.*

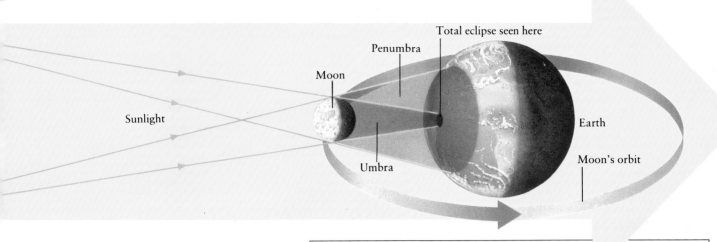

Total eclipse seen here
Penumbra
Moon
Sunlight
Umbra
Earth
Moon's orbit

▲ *The Moon casts a tapering shadow in space. When it passes between the Earth and the Sun, the shadow's tip may cross the Earth, causing an eclipse. Inside the shadow, the Sun is blocked from view, and all that can be seen in the dark sky is the Sun's corona. An eclipse is total only if seen from within the Moon's umbra, or central shadow. Inside the penumbra, or outer shadow, the Sun's disk is not completely hidden.*

Stream of atomic particles

TYPES OF ECLIPSE

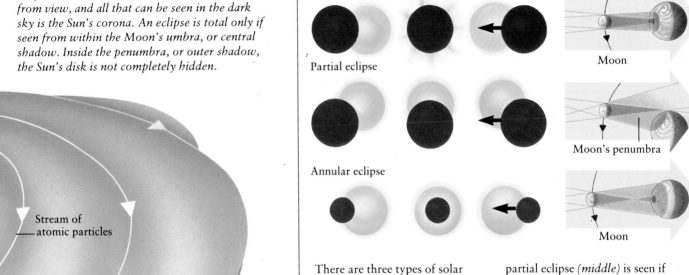

Total eclipse

Partial eclipse

Moon

Moon's penumbra

Annular eclipse

Moon

There are three types of solar eclipse. During a total eclipse *(top)* the Moon totally covers the Sun. This is visible from a narrow strip crossing the Earth's surface, usually about 90 mi. (150 km) wide. Beyond this strip a partial eclipse is seen. Only a partial eclipse *(middle)* is seen if the Moon's penumbra crosses Earth, instead of the umbra. An annular eclipse *(below)* happens when the Moon is at its greatest distance from Earth (called the apogee) and appears too small to cover the Sun completely.

▶ *The Sun gives out invisible radiation which can destroy living tissue. This radiation is filtered by a thin layer of ozone in the stratosphere before it reaches Earth. However, a "hole" in the layer, near the South Pole, has been caused by gases known as chlorofluorocarbons (CFCs). CFCs are now being banned.*

Radiation from Sun   Hole in ozone layer

Radiation blocked off

Some radiation gets through

Ozone layer

▲ *This plant has been affected by the kind of radiation usually blocked out by the ozone layer.*

17

The Planets

A planet is a large body, made of gas, metal, or rock, that orbits a star. We know of nine planets that orbit our Sun. All of them were formed at the same time, from the same cloud of gas and dust around the Sun, but there are great differences between them. The four inner terrestrial planets (Mercury, Venus, Earth, and Mars) are rock and metal. Jupiter, Saturn, Uranus, and Neptune are mainly liquid and ice; these giant outer bodies are the gaseous planets. Distant Pluto does not fit in either group.

THE DENSITY OF THE PLANETS

Compared with the gaseous planets, the inner rocky planets have no more than a thin skin of atmosphere. They contain much more material per unit of volume than the gaseous planets do, which means they are much denser. Water has a density of one gram per cubic centimeter. The Earth is five and a half times denser than water. Saturn, however, is *less* dense than water. It could float on a huge ocean.

▼ *Although Mercury is the innermost planet, it is not the hottest. It does have the shortest year, going around the Sun once every 88 days. It has a cratered surface and no satellites, or moons.*

▼ *Venus is the brightest object in the sky, but the planet is not shining by its own light. Venus is bright because the clouds that cover its surface reflect the Sun's light very well. All the planets shine by reflection.*

Mercury

Sun

Venus

Earth

Mars

Jupiter

▲ *The Earth is the only planet with liquid water on its surface. It is also the densest planet—almost eight times as dense as Saturn.*

▲ *The highest mountain and the deepest valleys in the Solar System are found on Mars, so it may once have been the most volcanically active planet.*

▲ *The largest planet, Jupiter, also spins fastest on its axis—its day lasts less than 10 Earth hours. This very rapid spin produces a force which makes the planet's liquid body bulge outward at the equator.*

MEASURING DISTANCES IN SPACE

Astronomers use special units to represent huge distances in space. These distances are measured in light-years: one light-year is equal to the distance traveled by a beam of light in one year, or 5.88 trillion mi. (9.46 trillion km). The basic unit of distance within our Solar System is the astronomical unit, or AU. One AU is the average distance from the Earth to the Sun —about 92,960,000 mi. (149,600,000 km).

| Mercury 0.39 AU | Venus 0.72 AU | Earth 1 AU | Mars 1.52 AU | Jupiter 5.20 AU | Saturn 9.54 AU | Uranus 19.19 AU |

0 1 2 3 4 5 6 7 8 9 10 11 12 13 14 15 16 17 18 19 20 21 22 23

FACTS ABOUT THE PLANETS

• We owe much of our knowledge about the Solar System to space probes. These unmanned spacecraft have investigated nearly every planet, sending back pictures to Earth. The *Voyager* probes were especially important. Between 1979 and 1989 the probes sent back close-up pictures of the four giant planets and their moons, and discovered rings around Jupiter, Uranus, and Neptune.

• Only Mercury and Venus have no natural satellites, or moons, at all. Saturn has the greatest number of moons: 18.
• The planets are named after ancient Greek and Roman gods; for example, Jupiter is named after the chief of the Roman gods.

• After the formation of the Solar System, leftover rocky debris in the cloud of particles around the Sun kept striking the planets as they formed. Mercury and our Moon still show the scars of impacts, but the Earth's craters have been smoothed out by weather and movements of the planet's surface. This main bombardment ended 3.9 billion years ago; some major impacts have occurred since.

▼ *Saturn used to be known as "the planet with the rings." Ring systems have now been discovered around all the giant planets, but Saturn's system is by far the largest and most complicated. Only Saturn's rings can be seen through a telescope from Earth.*

Uranus

◄ *Almost nothing was known about Uranus until the space probe* Voyager 2 *flew past it in 1986. Uranus's axis is tipped over so that it spins almost sideways.*

Pluto

Neptune

Saturn

▲ *Until 1999, Neptune will be the outermost planet in the Solar System, since Pluto's orbit has brought it briefly closer to the Sun. Neptune has a cold, windswept, cloudy surface.*

▲ *We know very little about distant Pluto, which was discovered only in 1930. It is the smallest planet, and is probably made of ice. No space probe has ever visited this mysterious world.*

Pluto 29.6 AU (at its closest)   Neptune 30.1 AU   Pluto 49.5 AU (at its farthest)

26 27 28 29 30 31 32 33 34 35 36 37 38 39 40 41 42 43 44 45 46 47 48 49 50

Mercury

Mercury is the innermost planet. It is a dead, airless world that whirls through space in the merciless glare of the Sun. The one spacecraft to have visited it was *Mariner 10* (in 1974), which photographed half the planet. During its daytime, which lasts for about three Earth months, it is so hot that lead would run like water over the rocks. But at night its surface is colder than icy Jupiter. Mercury holds two records for the major planets of the Solar System: the longest day and the shortest year.

▲ *Mercury is the second smallest of the planets, after Pluto. It is also smaller than two satellites, Jupiter's Ganymede and Saturn's Titan. Because it is so close to the Sun, it is bombarded by the solar wind. (Distances not to scale.)*

Earth

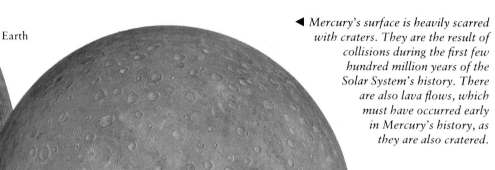

◀ *Mercury's surface is heavily scarred with craters. They are the result of collisions during the first few hundred million years of the Solar System's history. There are also lava flows, which must have occurred early in Mercury's history, as they are also cratered.*

▼ *Mercury's distance from the Sun changes as it rounds its orbit. From the planet's surface, the Sun would appear 1.5 times bigger when Mercury is closest than when it is farthest away.*

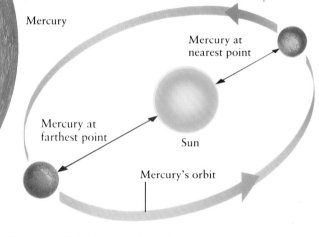

Mercury

Mercury at nearest point

Mercury at farthest point

Sun

Mercury's orbit

MERCURY DATAFILE

Diameter: 3,030 mi.
Mass: 0.06 × Earth
Density: 5.4 (water = 1)
Minimum distance from Sun:
  28.5 million mi.
Maximum distance from Sun:
  43.3 million mi.
Minimum distance from Earth:
  28 million mi.
Day/night: 176 Earth days
Length of year: 88 Earth days
Tilt of axis: 0° 0′
Surface gravity: 0.38 × Earth
Temperature: −300°F to 800°F
Satellites: 0

STRUCTURE

Extremely thin atmosphere
Crust
Rocky mantle
Huge iron-nickel core

FACTS ABOUT MERCURY

● The length of Mercury's year is shorter than its day. The planet has the shortest year in the Solar System—only 88 Earth days—but sunrise to sunrise on Mercury takes 176 Earth days.
● It is possible that some of Mercury's rocky mantle was knocked off by an impact with another body. Most of the interior is taken up by a huge iron core.

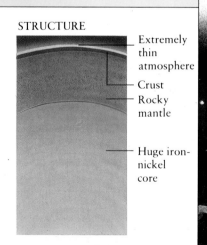

▲ *The smooth plains between the craters on Mercury suggest the planet might once have been a volcanic world. Following the formation of the Solar System, lava flows would have filled in the heavily cratered areas remaining after the bombardment of the planets.*

Impact with huge object

Shock waves travel through the planet

Caloris Basin, 800 miles across

Ridges form on the opposite side of Mercury

THE FORMATION OF THE CALORIS BASIN

The dominant feature on Mercury is the Caloris Basin. It is an ancient lava-filled crater about 800 mi. (1,300 km) across —a quarter of the planet's diameter. It is thought that the basin was formed when a huge body, about 60 mi. (100 km) across, crashed into Mercury. Shock waves from the collision traveled around the planet, meeting on the opposite point and throwing up a confusion of ridges. Half the Caloris Basin was in darkness when visited by *Mariner 10*, so that it has never been seen clearly.

▼ *There is practically no atmosphere on Mercury to reflect the light of the Sun, and so the sky is always black. The Sun takes about three of our months to pass across the sky, but some of the deepest craters have been in darkness for billions of years. The surface is crossed with huge wrinkle ridges, such as Discovery Rupes, 2 mi. (3 km) high and about 300 mi. (500 km) long.*

THE FORMATION OF RIDGES

Mercury is the second densest of all the planets, so it must have a large metallic core, presumably of iron. When heated or cooled, iron changes its size much more than rock. So as the hot core cooled over the hundreds of millions of years after the planet formed, it began to shrink, making the hard crust go loose and wrinkled like the skin on a dried apple. These wrinkle ridges are known as rupes, and are found all over Mercury. They are up to 2 mi. (3 km) high.

Crater

Core shrinks

Mantle and crust are squeezed as core shrinks

Core shrinks as it cools

Venus

Through a telescope Venus appears as a gleaming, silvery gem. But appearances deceive, because the planet is in fact a rocky waste, hotter than Mercury and spread out under a choking carbon dioxide atmosphere that is denser than water. Sulfuric acid droplets fall on the surface from clouds that permanently cast an orange gloom.
The surface features shown on these pages (mountains, craters, and volcanoes) were detected by spacecraft radar —the only way of probing the thick clouds.

▲ *Although the surface conditions are totally different, Venus is almost a twin of the Earth in size. Venus is very hot because its thick atmosphere is very efficient at holding in the Sun's heat. (Distances not to scale.)*

Earth   Venus

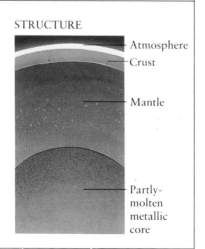

◄ *The orbit of Venus lies between the Earth and the Sun. This means it can be seen only in the twilight after sunset or before sunrise. Venus is sometimes called the morning star or the evening star.*

▼ *Venus's atmosphere is made up almost entirely of carbon dioxide, produced in vast amounts from erupting volcanoes when the planet was young. Sunlight penetrates the atmosphere and warms the surface of the planet. The ground radiates heat waves, but they cannot escape back into space because of the thick cloud layer. The heat is trapped, warming the planet still more.*

▲ *The surface of Venus is completely hidden by dense clouds.*

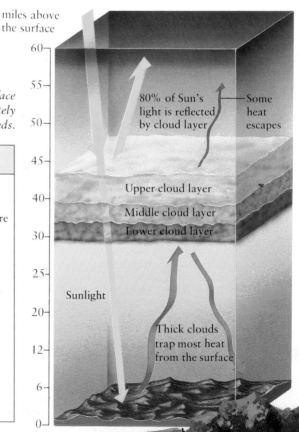

miles above the surface

80% of Sun's light is reflected by cloud layer — Some heat escapes

Upper cloud layer
Middle cloud layer
Lower cloud layer

Sunlight

Thick clouds trap most heat from the surface

VENUS DATAFILE

Diameter: 7,545 mi.
Mass: 0.82 × Earth
Density: 5.2 (water = 1)
Minimum distance from Sun:
   67 million mi.
Maximum distance from Sun:
   68 million mi.
Minimum distance from Earth:
   25 million mi.
Day/night: 117 Earth days
Length of year: 225 Earth days
Tilt of axis: 12° 42′
Surface gravity: 0.90 × Earth
Temperature: 900°F average
Satellites: 0

STRUCTURE

Atmosphere
Crust

Mantle

Partly-molten metallic core

ISHTAR TERRA
(highland area, as
large as Australia)

Cleopatra

Maxwell
Montes

ATLANTA
PLANITIA

GUINEVERE PLANITIA

SEDNA
PLANITIA

LEDA
PLANITIA

Rhea
Mons

Theia Mons

Sif
Mons

Gula
Mons

APHRODITE TERRA
(highland area, as
large as Africa)

LAVINIA
PLANITIA

◄ *An artist's
impression of Venus's
surface, based on
radar information. The
highland areas, or
continents, are
colored yellow. The
mountain Maxwell
Montes is 7 mi. (12 km)
high. Its peaks are the
second highest in the
Solar System. About
80 percent of the
surface of Venus is
covered with dusty,
rocky lava plains,
which have smothered
most of the early
craters. A well-known
crater, Cleopatra, is
100 mi. (160 km) across.*

► *The* Magellan
*spacecraft mapped 99
percent of the surface
of Venus in 1990–
1992. It recorded
features as small in
size as a football field.*

◄ *Maat Mons is a
volcanic feature on
Venus, 5 mi. (8 km)
high. Radar information
from* Magellan *was
processed by computer
technology to produce
this image.*

► *Sulfur dioxide
from early volcanic
activity has helped to
form dense sulfuric
acid clouds. These
spread in a corrosive
mist over the surface
of Venus.*

The Earth

As far as we know, the Earth is unique in the Solar System for two reasons: it has liquid water on its surface, and it supports life. Both are probably dependent on each other. Without water, the type of plant life we know could not have flourished; without plant life, oxygen would not have been released into the early carbon dioxide atmosphere to make air for animals to breathe. A permanent carbon dioxide covering might have created a similar atmosphere to that on Venus, turning Earth's surface into a desert.

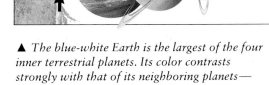

▲ The blue-white Earth is the largest of the four inner terrestrial planets. Its color contrasts strongly with that of its neighboring planets—jewel-bright Venus and reddish Mars. (Distances not to scale.)

▼ The Earth's atmosphere is about 78 percent nitrogen, 21 percent oxygen, and 1 percent other gases. Half of the Earth's atmospheric material is found in the troposphere, 6 mi. (10 km) high. The stratosphere contains the ozone layer which absorbs dangerous ultraviolet rays from the Sun. The mesosphere is where meteoroids, or small space bodies, burn up because of air resistance.

Earth

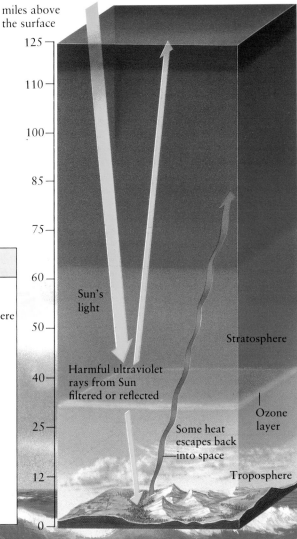

miles above the surface

Sun's light

Harmful ultraviolet rays from Sun filtered or reflected

Some heat escapes back into space

Stratosphere

Ozone layer

Troposphere

EARTH DATAFILE

Diameter: 7,926 mi.
Mass: 6.5 sextillion tons
Density: 5.5 (water = 1)
Minimum distance from Sun: 91 million mi.
Maximum distance from Sun: 94.5 million mi.
Day/night: 24 h
Length of year: 365 days 5 h
Tilt of axis: 23° 27′
True rotation period: 23 h 56 min
Maximum temperature: 136°F
Minimum temperature: −128°F
Satellites: 1

STRUCTURE

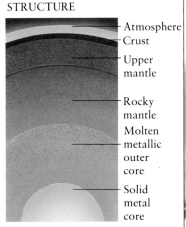

- Atmosphere
- Crust
- Upper mantle
- Rocky mantle
- Molten metallic outer core
- Solid metal core

Circular orbit

Sun

Elongated orbit

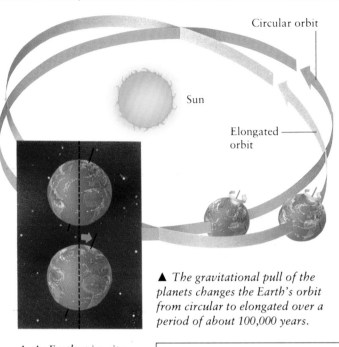

▲ As Earth spins, its axis slowly rotates. One complete rotation takes 25,800 years. This is known as precession.

▲ *The gravitational pull of the planets changes the Earth's orbit from circular to elongated over a period of about 100,000 years.*

▶ *The Earth has had a number of Ice Ages, the last one thousands of years ago. These may have been caused by changes in the shape of the Earth's orbit and the tilt of its axis. Today, summers are warm and winters cool. But changes to the Earth's orbit and tilt could mean that the temperature hardly changes and winter snow does not melt in the summer. Instead, ice reflects the Sun's radiation back into space, the temperature falls further, and an Ice Age begins.*

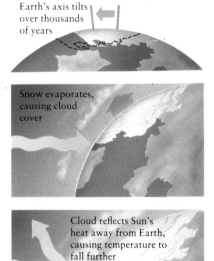

Earth's axis tilts over thousands of years

Snow evaporates, causing cloud cover

Cloud reflects Sun's heat away from Earth, causing temperature to fall further

▼ *The Earth's surface water is in a delicate balance. Vapor rises from the sea, condenses as clouds, and falls back as rain or snow.*

THE CHANGING SURFACE

The crust of the Earth is not an unbroken shell; it is made up of several giant plates of solid rock. The plates are floating on the moving molten rock of the Earth's mantle beneath. The Earth's surface is constantly changing because of the great forces created by these plates as they drift. If two plates move against each other the crust may be forced up in mountain chains. An example is the Andes chain, which runs down South America. In the middle of the oceans, ridges form where the sea floor is spreading, as rock from the mantle wells up and forms new crust. The ridge marks the edge of a plate.

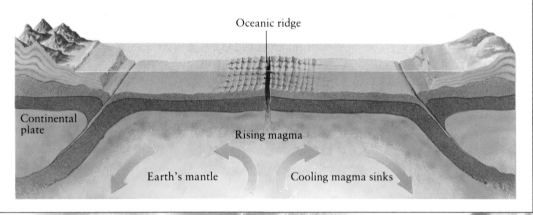

Oceanic ridge

Continental plate

Rising magma

Earth's mantle

Cooling magma sinks

The Moon

The Moon is the Earth's satellite, a pitted rocky body
orbiting our planet. It has no light of its own, but seems
bright in the sky because it reflects the light of the Sun.
The Moon is a fossilized world, where little has happened
during the last 3 billion years—but it has had a violent
past. The Moon's surface was cratered by bodies that
crashed into it between 3 and 4 billion years ago, exploding
on the surface. The craters have not worn away, but
display the Moon's history for all to see.

▼ *The diameter of the Moon is
roughly equal to the
distance across
Australia.*

▲ *The crater Eratosthenes measures 38 mi.
(61 km) across. It must have been formed after
the surrounding lava plains, otherwise it would
have been melted down by the flood of hot rock.*

◄ *The side of the Moon turned toward
Earth has huge lava plains, called
maria. The pull of Earth's gravity
strained and weakened this side,
pulling it out of shape. As a result,
lava flowed out through cracks
in the crust, flooding the older
craters to form lava plains.*

BAY OF RAINBOWS

SEA OF SHOWERS

SEA OF SERENITY

Eratosthenes

SEA OF CRISES

OCEAN OF STORMS

SEA OF TRANQUILLITY

Copernicus

SEA OF FERTILITY

SEA OF CLOUDS

SEA OF NECTAR

SEA OF MOISTURE

HUMBOLDT'S SEA

SOUTHERN SEA

MOON DATAFILE

STRUCTURE

Crust

Mantle

Partially
molten
outer
core

Small,
iron-rich
core

Diameter: 2,160 mi.
Mass: 0.01 x Earth
Density: 3.3 (water = 1)
Minimum distance from Earth:
 221,000 mi.
Maximum distance from Earth:
 253,000 mi.
Day/night: 29.5 Earth days
True time to orbit Earth:
 27.3 Earth days
Lunar month (cycle of phases):
 29.5 Earth days
True rotation period: 27.3 days
Maximum temperature: 230°F
Minimum temperature: −274°F

◄ *The far side of the Moon
is covered with craters and
mountain ranges. The lunar
mountains were not caused by
crustal movements but are the
surviving walls of huge, ancient
craters. With no Earth shining
in the sky, the nights must be
very dark indeed.*

HOW THE CRATERS WERE FORMED

Most of the craters on the Moon were formed when smaller bodies, a few miles across, crashed into its surface. A body striking the surface of the Moon at a speed greater than 6 mi./s (10 km/s) would explode, blasting out a crater about 10 times its own width. Silica, a glassy substance found in rock, might be sprayed out for hundreds of miles. The silica would form bright rays, extending out of the crater. The violent impact on the floor of the crater would create a shock wave, making the floor spring back up as a central mountain.

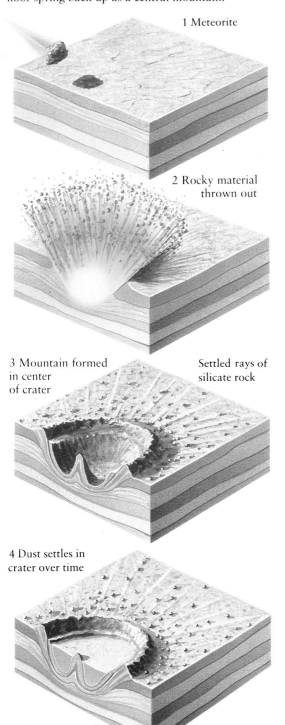

1 Meteorite

2 Rocky material thrown out

3 Mountain formed in center of crater

Settled rays of silicate rock

4 Dust settles in crater over time

MOON ROCKS

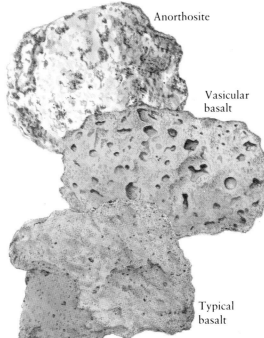

Anorthosite

Vasicular basalt

Typical basalt

▲ *The U.S. Apollo project answered a number of questions about the Moon, confirming that its surface is firm and the core is still hot.*

◀ *Compared with Earth rocks, the samples brought back from the Moon by the Apollo project contain more of some elements such as titanium, and less of others such as gold. The ages of the Moon rock samples range from about 4.5 billion years (not long after the birth of the Moon) to 3.1 billion years— the time when the lava plains formed.*

FACTS ABOUT THE MOON

● The Moon has no atmosphere, and so there is no wind or weather either. As a result, the astronauts' footprints will last for centuries.
● Today, laser beams can measure the distance to the Moon with an accuracy of about 4 in. (10 cm).

The Earth and the Moon

It would be hard to imagine two rocky worlds more different than the Earth and the Moon—yet they orbit each other almost as a double planet. Most satellites are much smaller than the planet controlling them, but the diameter of the Moon is a quarter of the Earth's diameter. The Moon is a very useful body for us, illuminating half the nights every month as it reflects the Sun's light. Yet it may also block the light sent from the Sun during a solar eclipse, casting a black shadow on part of the Earth.

THE FORMATION OF THE MOON

Despite the closeness of the Moon to the Earth, we are still unable to say for certain how our satellite formed. A century ago it was believed that the molten Earth, spinning very fast, became unstable and threw a large blob of material into orbit. This theory has now been abandoned because, for this to happen, the Earth would have to spin once in only two and a half hours, which seems impossible. Three other theories have been put forward; they are illustrated here.

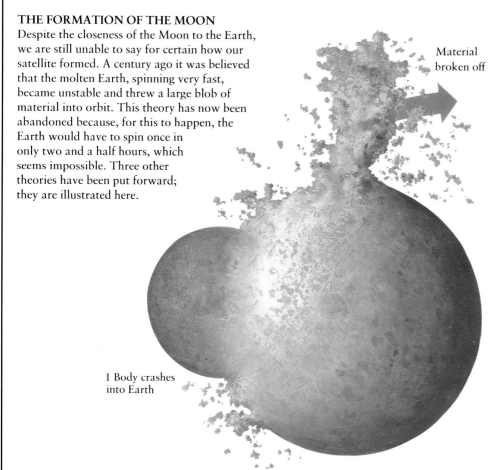

Material broken off

1 Body crashes into Earth

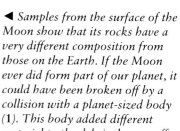

2

3

4

◀ *Samples from the surface of the Moon show that its rocks have a very different composition from those on the Earth. If the Moon ever did form part of our planet, it could have been broken off by a collision with a planet-sized body (1). This body added different material to the debris thrown off into space (2). The debris formed an orbiting cloud (3) which finally condensed into the Moon (4).*

◀ *The Earth and the Moon may have formed together as a double planet from the cloud of debris left over after the formation of the Sun. This idea is attractive because it does not assume an unlikely event, such as a collision. But if the two bodies formed so closely together, why are their surface rocks so different? And why does the Moon have such a small iron core compared with the Earth's?*

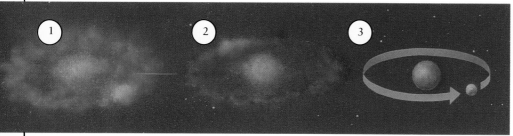

1

2

3

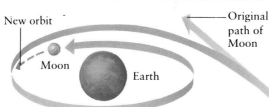

New orbit

Original path of Moon

Moon

Earth

▶ *The capture theory assumes that the Moon was a passing body caught by the Earth's gravity. This explains its different composition. However, calculations show that a capture is far less likely than a collision with another body.*

◀ In this photograph, taken by Apollo 11, the blue-and-white Earth contrasts with the bare lunar surface. The Moon's weak gravity could not hold on to any atmosphere, and so it became just a huge ball of stone, exposed to fierce temperature extremes of day and night. The photo is often called "Earthrise." However, this is not accurate. The Earth never rises or sets in the Moon's sky, since the same hemisphere of the Moon is always turned toward the Earth.

THE PHASES OF THE MOON

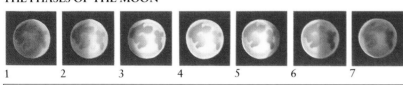

1   2   3   4   5   6   7

◀ At New Moon, the unlit side of the Moon is toward the Earth, so it is invisible. As it moves through the first quarter of its orbit, a crescent moon (1), half (2), and then nearly all the unlit side (3) are seen. At Full Moon the sunlit side faces the Earth, and the Moon appears round (4). The phases then continue in the reverse order until the Moon is new again (5, 6, 7). The phase cycle takes 29.5 days—the lunar month.

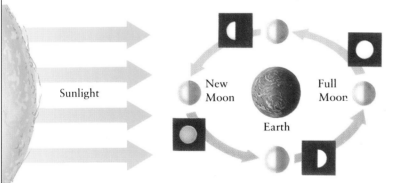

Sunlight

New Moon

Full Moon

Earth

ECLIPSE OF THE MOON
The Full Moon sometimes passes through the Earth's shadow. The Moon does not become invisible, because a little sunlight is diffused into the shadow by the Earth's atmosphere.

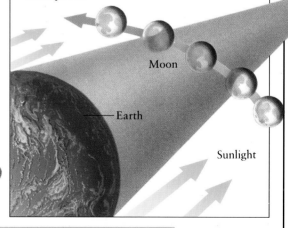

Moon

Earth

Sunlight

▶ Because the Moon has an elliptical orbit it is not always the same distance from the Earth. The point when the Moon is at its closest to the Earth is called its perigee. The point when the Moon is farthest from the Earth is its apogee.

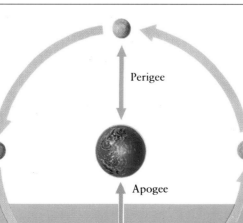

Perigee

Apogee

Earth

Perigee 221,462 mi.   Moon

Earth

Apogee 252,718 mi.   Moon

Mars

This mysterious planet has intrigued skywatchers for centuries. It shines very brightly when closest to the Earth, moving quickly in front of the stars, and it has a bright, reddish color. Less than a century ago, many people believed in Martians, and the possibility of finding some kind of life form inspired the *Viking* missions in 1976. Although apparently dead and inhospitable, Mars is the only planet selected for possible human exploration, and further visits by unmanned spacecraft are planned.

▲ *Mars is the outermost of the rocky planets. A vast gap, twice the diameter of its own orbit, separates Mars from Jupiter. Most of the asteroids, or minor planets, are found in this gap. (Distances not to scale.)*

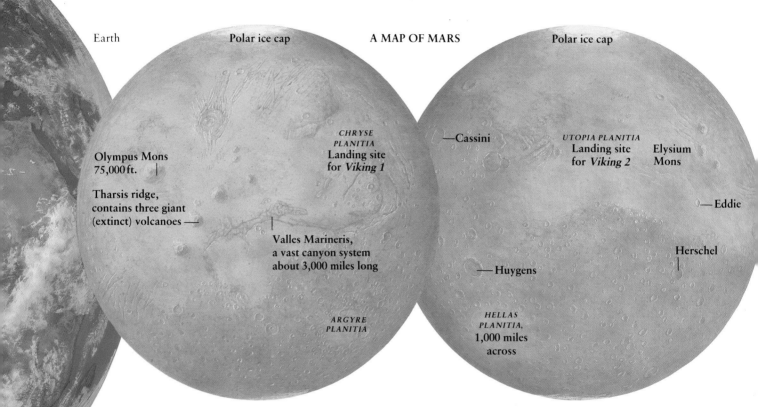

Earth

Polar ice cap

A MAP OF MARS

Polar ice cap

Olympus Mons 75,000 ft.

Tharsis ridge, contains three giant (extinct) volcanoes —

CHRYSE PLANITIA
Landing site for *Viking 1*

Valles Marineris, a vast canyon system about 3,000 miles long

ARGYRE PLANITIA

—Cassini

UTOPIA PLANITIA
Landing site for *Viking 2*

Elysium Mons

—Eddie

Herschel

—Huygens

HELLAS PLANITIA,
1,000 miles across

MARS DATAFILE

Diameter: 4,217 mi.
Mass: 0.11 × Earth
Density: 3.9 (water = 1)
Minimum distance from Sun: 128 million mi.
Maximum distance from Sun: 155 million mi.
Minimum distance from Earth: 35 million mi.
Day/night: 24 h 37 min
Length of year: 687 Earth days
Tilt of axis: 25° 12′
Surface gravity: 0.38 × Earth
Temperature: −116°F to 32°F
Satellites: 2

STRUCTURE

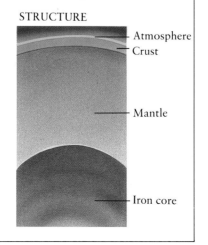

Atmosphere
Crust

Mantle

Iron core

MARTIAN ATMOSPHERE

Mars's atmosphere is primarily carbon dioxide, with nitrogen, argon, and small amounts of other gases. At 20 mi. (30 km) up, winds can raise huge dust-clouds. At night, carbon dioxide freezes on parts of the surface as hoar frost. Traces of water can form thin hazes at dusk and dawn.

Thick cloud layer

Carbon dioxide gas

Dust clouds

SATELLITES OF MARS

Deimos is about 7 mi. (11 km) long, and covered with small craters. From Mars, Deimos would appear as an almost star-like object, remaining above the horizon for two nights at a time.

Deimos

Phobos

Phobos is larger and closer to Mars than Deimos. It is about 12 mi. (19 km) long. It orbits Mars in only seven and a half hours, so that it rises in the west, and then sets in the east about four hours later.

▲ *This view of the surface of Mars was taken by the* Viking 2 *lander (left). It shows a desert of rocks, each up to about 12 in. (30 cm) across, under an orange sky.*

▼ *The color of Mars's sky comes from wind-borne dust blown from the reddish surface. Early in the planet's history, when it was warmer and damp, the iron-rich surface rusted, turning Mars into a red planet.*

Viking Lander

FACTS ABOUT MARS

● About 4 billion years ago, Mars may have been warm enough for water to run in rivers over its surface.
● Phobos, the inner moon, goes around the planet three times while Mars spins on its axis once. This means that Phobos's "month" is shorter than Mars's day.
● The Valles Marineris is an enormous canyon system running for some 2,500 mi. (4,000 km) along the surface of Mars. In some places it is 4 mi. (6 km) deep.
● Did a *Viking* orbiter record a landslide on Mars in 1978? Two close-up pictures of part of the Valles Marineris, taken two and a half minutes apart, appear to show a sudden cloud of dust 2,000 ft. (600 m) high.

▶ *Roughly half of the Martian surface shows signs of past volcanic activity. The volcanic mountain Olympus Mons rises 14 mi. (23 km) above the plain. It is the highest peak in the Solar System and shows how violent the volcanic activity must have been. Elsewhere on Mars, there are winding valleys that look just like dried-up river beds.*

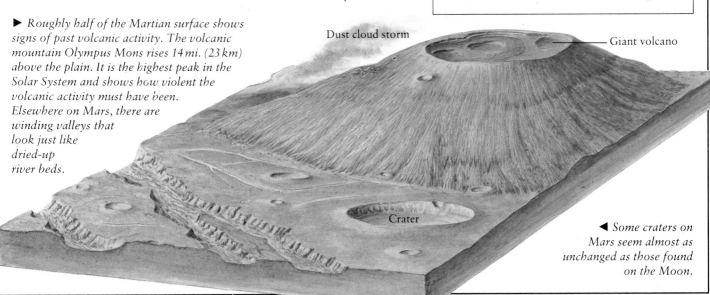

Dust cloud storm

Giant volcano

Crater

◀ *Some craters on Mars seem almost as unchanged as those found on the Moon.*

Jupiter

Jupiter is by far the largest planet in the Solar System—it is so huge that all the other planets could be squeezed inside it. It spins faster than any of the other planets, too, so that its day lasts less than 10 hours. Jupiter is made up of about 90 percent hydrogen and 10 percent helium, with traces of other elements. Its core must be hotter than the surface of the Sun, but the clouds exposed to space are bitterly cold. Its vivid stripes are cloud markings, drawn out into dark belts and light zones by Jupiter's rapid spin.

▲ *Although Jupiter is the largest planet, it has only a thousandth of the Sun's mass. Even the smallest and dimmest known stars contain about a hundred times as much material as Jupiter. (Distances not to scale.)*

▶ *The details of Jupiter's appearance are always changing. The cloud belts are caused by clouds of frozen ammonia, ammonium hydrosulfide, water ice, and other compounds being swept through the outer layers of the planet at up to 250 mph (400 km/h). Some markings have lasted for decades.*

Earth

Jupiter

▶ *The Great Red Spot is a vast whirlpool on the surface of Jupiter. About twice the Earth's diameter, it draws material up from below as it rotates every six days. This cloud feature has been observed for a century, and possibly longer. The color, which sometimes fades away for several years, may be caused by sunlight reacting with chemicals in the clouds to release red phosphorus.*

▲ *Jupiter's ring is about 4,000 mi. wide and 20 mi. thick. It is surrounded by a fainter 12,500-mi.-wide halo. The ring is made up of particles which measure about 0.01 mm across. Another ring of sulfur particles lies in Io's orbit.*

JUPITER DATAFILE

Diameter: 88,700 mi.
Mass: 318 × Earth
Density: 1.3 (water = 1)
Minimum distance from Sun:
  460 million mi.
Maximum distance from Sun:
  507 million mi.
Minimum distance from Earth:
  367 million mi.
Day/night: 9 h 50 min (equator)
Length of year: 11.9 Earth years
Tilt of axis: 3°
Surface gravity: 2.7 × Earth
Temperature: −238°F
Satellites: 16 known

STRUCTURE

Atmosphere

Liquid hydrogen

Liquid metallic hydrogen

Iron core

JUPITER'S ATMOSPHERE

Jupiter's clouds lie in the upper 150 mi. (200 km) of the atmosphere—less than one percent of the distance to the center. The planet is made up of almost pure hydrogen and helium, compressed to a fiercely hot liquid. This churning liquid generates a powerful magnetic field and electrical currents, which produce radio waves.

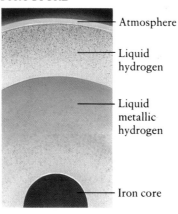

Tops of clouds

Hydrogen gas

Crystals of ammonia ice

Clouds of ammonium sulfide

Droplets of water ice

Liquid hydrogen

EXPLORING JUPITER

The *Galileo* probe should reach Jupiter in 1995. The main craft will study the planet and its satellites. A probe will be released into Jupiter's atmosphere to record the conditions and chemical make-up of the outer layers, before the probe is destroyed by the fierce pressure. *Galileo* was launched in 1989. It used the gravity of Venus and the Earth to speed it on its way to Jupiter.

Flyby Earth (1), 1990

Flyby Earth (2), 1992

Flyby Venus, 1990

Galileo launch, 1989

Arrives at Jupiter, 1995

Galileo probe

THE GALILEAN SATELLITES

Jupiter's four large satellites were discovered by Galileo Galilei (1564–1642) with his primitive telescope in 1610. They include Ganymede, the largest satellite in the Solar System. Although the satellites can be seen using binoculars, the *Voyager* spacecraft produced our first detailed view of their surfaces in 1979. *(Their sizes are shown to scale here.)*

◄ *Callisto, the outermost Galilean satellite, is covered with ancient craters. However, unlike our Moon, it shows no sign of any later lava flows. All the satellites keep the same face turned inward toward Jupiter.*

▲ *Ganymede is the largest satellite in the Solar System, 3,270 mi. (5,262 km) across. Parts of its crust may have drifted over the hot rock beneath, as happened on Earth.*

A volcano explodes on Io

► *Europa is covered in ice many miles thick, making it the smoothest known body anywhere. The dark streaks may be fractures in the surface, filled with ice.*

► *Io is a sulfur-covered volcanic world. Constant eruptions shoot material 125 mi. (200 km) into space before it falls back onto the orange-yellow surface.*

Saturn

Saturn has been known for centuries as the ringed planet. In fact, due to the *Voyager* space probes we now know that all four giant planets have rings, though Saturn's rings are by far the most impressive. There is less cloud detail visible on Saturn than on Jupiter. This may be because a layer of haze makes it hard to see what cloud belts lie lower down. However, about three times every century violent storms disturb the calm surface and cause brilliant white "spots" to break out on the planet.

▲ *Like the other giant planets, Saturn spins so quickly that its equator now bulges outward noticeably. This gives the planet a slightly squashed look. The bulge is due to centrifugal force. (Distances not to scale.)*

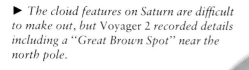

▶ *The cloud features on Saturn are difficult to make out, but* Voyager 2 *recorded details including a "Great Brown Spot" near the north pole.*

▶ *Under this calm-looking surface, material is being swept around at speeds of up to 1,120 mph (1,800 km/h). In 1990 a huge white eruption was easily visible from Earth through telescopes.*

Earth

Saturn

▲ *Saturn's rings extend for over 46,000 mi. (74,000 km), but are only a few miles deep. Although they seem to be several wide zones, they are really thousands of separate narrow ringlets. The rings could be the remains of a small satellite, 60 mi. (100 km) across.*

Cassini division

▲ *The Cassini Division is a wide zone in the rings where the particles are scattered. They have been pulled into different orbits by Saturn's moons.*

SATURN'S ATMOSPHERE
The cloud layers form a skin as thin as apple peel over the hydrogen and helium body of Saturn. *Voyager 2* had a much clearer view of the cloud formations than *Voyager 1* did, when it passed nine months earlier. This suggests that the upper ammonia haze varies in transparency.

SATURN DATAFILE

Diameter: 74,500 mi.
Mass: 95 × Earth
Density: 0.7 (water = 1)
Minimum distance from Sun:
  840 million mi.
Maximum distance from Sun:
  938 million mi.
Minimum distance from Earth:
  746 million mi.
Day/night: 10 h 14 min (equator)
Length of year: 29.5 Earth years
Tilt of axis: 26° 42'
Surface gravity: 1.2 × Earth
Temperature: −274°F
Satellites: 18 known

STRUCTURE

- Atmosphere
- Liquid hydrogen
- Liquid metallic hydrogen
- Iron core

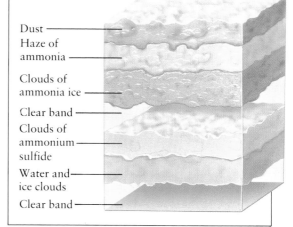

- Dust
- Haze of ammonia
- Clouds of ammonia ice
- Clear band
- Clouds of ammonium sulfide
- Water and ice clouds
- Clear band

▲ *The* Cassini *spacecraft will be launched in 1997 and is planned to reach Saturn in 2002. It will orbit Saturn and study Titan, the largest moon. A probe will be dropped into Titan's atmosphere.*

SATURN'S SATELLITES

Saturn has more moons than any other planet. There are 18 satellites confirmed; 12 were discovered by the *Voyager* probes. The existence of other satellites is suspected. The moons range from the second largest in the Solar System (Titan, 3,200 mi. [5,150 km] across) to the second smallest (Pan, at 12 mi. [20 km] across, is slightly larger than Mars's Deimos). Titan is the only moon in the Solar System to have its own thick atmosphere, which makes it a prime target for the *Cassini* mission. Phoebe is the farthest moon from the planet, orbiting at 8 million mi. (13 million km) away.

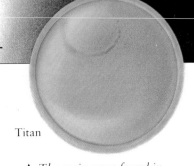

Titan

▲ *The main gases found in Titan's thick orange atmosphere are nitrogen and methane, with traces of organic compounds including ethane and acetylene. These compounds form the crude beginnings of molecules found in living cells. Titan's hidden surface could be a deep-frozen record of how more advanced organic molecules formed naturally out of simple gases.*

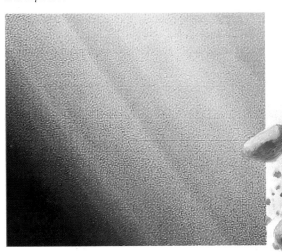

▲ Voyager 1 *visited Saturn in 1980. It sent back this image of the unique oval red cloud feature in Saturn's southern hemisphere.*

▶ *Saturn's rings are made up of billions of particles in orbit around the planet, ranging in size from grains to large rocks.*

RINGS AND SHEPHERD MOONS

Only rings A, B, and C are visible from the Earth. The particles in the brightest ring, B, seem to be icy. Calculations suggest that ice would eventually be dulled by fine space dust. Since this has not yet happened, the rings are probably less than a billion years old. The gravity of tiny satellites, known as shepherd moons, appears to control the position of some of the orbiting particles. For example, Prometheus and Pandora, each less than 93 mi. (150 km) across, orbit on either side of the narrow F ring.

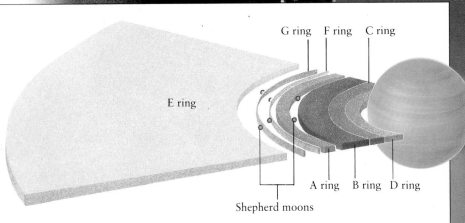

E ring
G ring F ring C ring
A ring B ring D ring
Shepherd moons

Uranus

Before the last decade, chance played a large part in our understanding of Uranus. Barely visible with the naked eye, the planet was discovered by accident in 1781. Two centuries later its faint ring system was also discovered by accident. Apart from the fact that it orbits the Sun on its side and has a family of satellites, little else was known. In the course of a few days in January 1986, pictures taken by the space probe *Voyager 2* transformed our knowledge of this remote giant.

▲ *Uranus has the volume of more than 60 Earths. The tilt of its axis means that its "north" pole is pointing slightly south. Uranus has a backward, or retrograde, spin—as do Venus and Pluto. (Distances not to scale.)*

Earth

Voyager 2

Uranus

DISCOVERING URANUS

Uranus was discovered by William Herschel (1738–1822), a musician from Germany who settled in Bath, England, and became fascinated by astronomy. In 1781 he was looking at the sky with his homemade telescope when he noticed a "star" that showed a small disk. The discovery earned Herschel royal recognition.

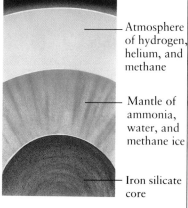

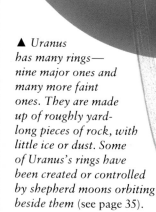

▲ *Uranus has many rings— nine major ones and many more faint ones. They are made up of roughly yard-long pieces of rock, with little ice or dust. Some of Uranus's rings have been created or controlled by shepherd moons orbiting beside them (see page 35).*

URANUS DATAFILE

Diameter: 32,000 mi.
Mass: 14.5 × Earth's mass
Density: 1.3 (water = 1)
Minimum distance from Sun:
   1.7 billion mi.
Maximum distance from Sun:
   1.87 billion mi.
Minimum distance from Earth:
   1.6 billion mi.
Day/night: 17 h 14 min
Length of year: 84 Earth years
Tilt of axis: 82°
Surface gravity: 0.93 × Earth
Temperature: −328°F
Satellites: 15

STRUCTURE

Atmosphere of hydrogen, helium, and methane

Mantle of ammonia, water, and methane ice

Iron silicate core

▶ *The strange tilt of Uranus may be the result of a collision with another large body, soon after Uranus had formed. The effect is that each pole spends about 40 years in constant summer sunlight, and then another 40 in continuous winter darkness. At the present time, one of the poles is almost facing the Sun. However, Voyager 2 took measurements that showed that the winter side was not as cold as expected, because of heat flowing back from the sunlit face.*

Direction of Uranus's rotation

Axis

Sun

Orbit

Miranda

Ariel

Titania

THE SATELLITES OF URANUS

Five satellites were known from Earth-based observation, but *Voyager* discovered 10 more, each less than 62 mi. (100 km) across. Unlike most Solar System satellites, which have mythological names, those of Uranus are named for Shakespearean characters such as Desdemona, Portia, and Oberon.

▼ *Very few craters can be seen on Miranda, which suggests that it formed after the main bombardment of craters (see page 19). It is possible that the original moon broke up and the pieces came together again.*

▶ *Miranda is 300 mi. (480 km) across, a curious, patchwork moon. There may be ice-cliffs on its surface towering 12 mi. (20 km) high.*

▶ *The surface of Ariel has few craters. It is possible that old, large craters have been melted down by volcanic activity in the past.*

▲ *Uranus's largest satellite, Titania, is an ice-covered world. Long valleys cross a landscape of craters, which measure up to 250 mi. (400 km) across.*

▼ *From Miranda's strange surface, Uranus looms vast in the black sky. Only when its equator is edge-on to the Sun will the planet appear completely sunlit.*

Neptune

Neptune was discovered in 1846 as a result of the effect of its gravitational pull on Uranus. Its brilliant blue methane atmosphere looks calm and cold (it has a temperature of −346°F [−210°C]). But *Voyager 2* discovered winds ripping through Neptune's atmosphere at 1,400 mph (2,200 km/h), the fiercest winds in the Solar System. The winds travel in a different direction to the planet's spin. Neptune's large satellite, Triton, the coldest land surface in the Solar System, has plumes of gas erupting into space.

▲ *Neptune is a little smaller than Uranus. It is the outermost giant planet, and for 20 years in every 250 years, when Pluto comes closest to the Sun (as in 1979–1999), it is also the outermost planet.* (Distances not to scale.)

Earth

► *Methane gas, which reflects blue light well, gives Neptune its intense color.*

Neptune

► Voyager 2 *found four faint rings around Neptune. The three brighter rings have been called Galle, Adams, and Leverrier, after the three people involved in the discovery of Neptune.*

◄ *Some cloud features appear and vanish in just a few minutes, rising up from the warmer layers and sinking again as they cool down. Long-lasting features, such as the Great Dark Spot and some of the white clouds, are being forced along by fierce currents.*

▲ *Neptune's rings are very narrow. Galle is 9 mi. (15 km) wide, and Adams, the widest, is less than 30 mi. (50 km) across.*

NEPTUNE DATAFILE

Diameter: 30,760 mi.
Mass: 17.2 × Earth
Density: 1.8 (water = 1)
Minimum distance from Sun:
   2.77 billion mi.
Maximum distance from Sun:
   2.82 billion mi.
Minimum distance from Earth:
   2.68 billion mi.
Day/night: 17 h 6 min
Length of year: 165 Earth years
Tilt of axis: 29° 36′
Surface gravity: 1.2 × Earth
Temperature: −346°F
Satellites: 8

STRUCTURE

Atmosphere of hydrogen, helium, and methane

Icy mantle

Iron core

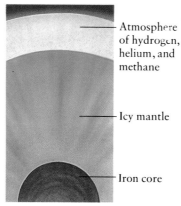

Leverrier

▲ *The Sun's gravity rules the planets, but their own much weaker gravity also pulls at each other. The independent calculations of John Couch Adams in England and Urbain Leverrier in France in 1845 showed that an unknown planet was pulling Uranus from its true path. These calculations led to the discovery of Neptune by Johann Galle in Germany.*

▶ *The Great Dark Spot was discovered by* Voyager 2. *Large enough to contain the Earth, the spot changes in size and shape as the material inside it is slowly churned around once every 16 days. A much smaller dark spot, known as D2, was also seen in Neptune's southern hemisphere; both spots were observed for several weeks.*

SATELLITES OF NEPTUNE

Neptune has eight satellites, six of them discovered by *Voyager 2.* The five tiny inner satellites orbit Neptune faster than it spins. The next, Proteus, is 258 mi. (415 km) across. Nereid, the small outermost satellite discovered from Earth, takes a year to make one orbit, sweeping close to Neptune and then far out into space, like a comet.

Nereid

Triton

Proteus

TRITON

The largest of Neptune's satellites, Triton, is 1,681 mi. (2,705 km) across, with a crust of rock-hard ice at a temperature of −391°F (−235°C). Although its gravity is too weak to hold a proper atmosphere, a thin layer of nitrogen is fed by plumes of gas from the surface. Triton orbits Neptune backward; this suggests that the satellite was captured by the planet's gravity, or suffered a space accident that altered its path.

▲ *This close-up of Triton's south pole was taken by* Voyager 2. *The probe was only 120,000 mi. (190,000 km) from Triton's surface. The white material may be frost; the long dark streaks may be dust, blown by winds.*

39

Pluto and Beyond

Uranus and Neptune have slightly erratic orbits. The cause of this was suspected to be the pull of gravity from a ninth planet. This led to the discovery of Pluto in 1930 during a thorough search of the sky for "Planet X" by the American astronomer Clyde Tombaugh. We still know very little about Pluto. It is the only planet we have not observed in close-up from a spacecraft and is too far away to see in detail with a telescope.

▲ *Tiny Pluto, on the frontier of the Solar System, is smaller than our Moon and only twice the diameter of the largest asteroid. Its eccentric orbit carries it closer than Neptune to the Sun at perihelion. (Distances not to scale.)*

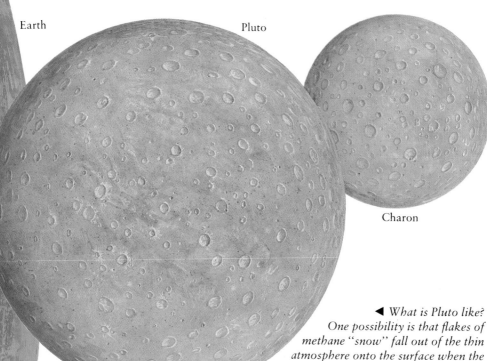

Earth

Pluto

Charon

◀ *No telescope has seen Pluto, or its moon Charon, in detail. Charon was detected from Earth in 1978. It is about half the size of Pluto, with a diameter of 750 mi. (1,200 km). Pluto and Charon orbit each other like a double planet. Each one keeps the same hemisphere facing toward the other, and at certain periods during Pluto's year Charon is eclipsed at each revolution.*

◀ *What is Pluto like? One possibility is that flakes of methane "snow" fall out of the thin atmosphere onto the surface when the planet swings far away from the Sun and the surface temperature falls. When it approaches perihelion again, the increasing warmth turns the methane snow back into gas, and the atmosphere is restored.*

▼ *The clearest image we have of Pluto and Charon comes from the HST (see pages 70–71). The photo shows their relative sizes, but they are farther apart than it appears here.*

PLUTO DATAFILE

Diameter: 1,430 mi.
Mass: 0.002 × Earth
Density: Approx 2 (water = 1)
Minimum distance from Sun:
  2.7 billion mi.
Maximum distance from Sun:
  4.6 billion mi.
Minimum distance from Earth:
  2.7 billion mi.
Day/night: 6 Earth d 9 h
Length of year: 248 Earth years
Tilt of axis: 62° 24′
Surface gravity: 0.03 × Earth
Temperature: −380°F
Satellites: 1

STRUCTURE

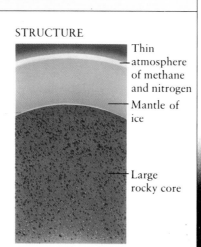

Thin atmosphere of methane and nitrogen

Mantle of ice

Large rocky core

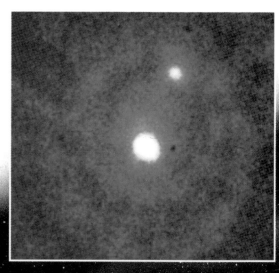

PLUTO'S ORBIT

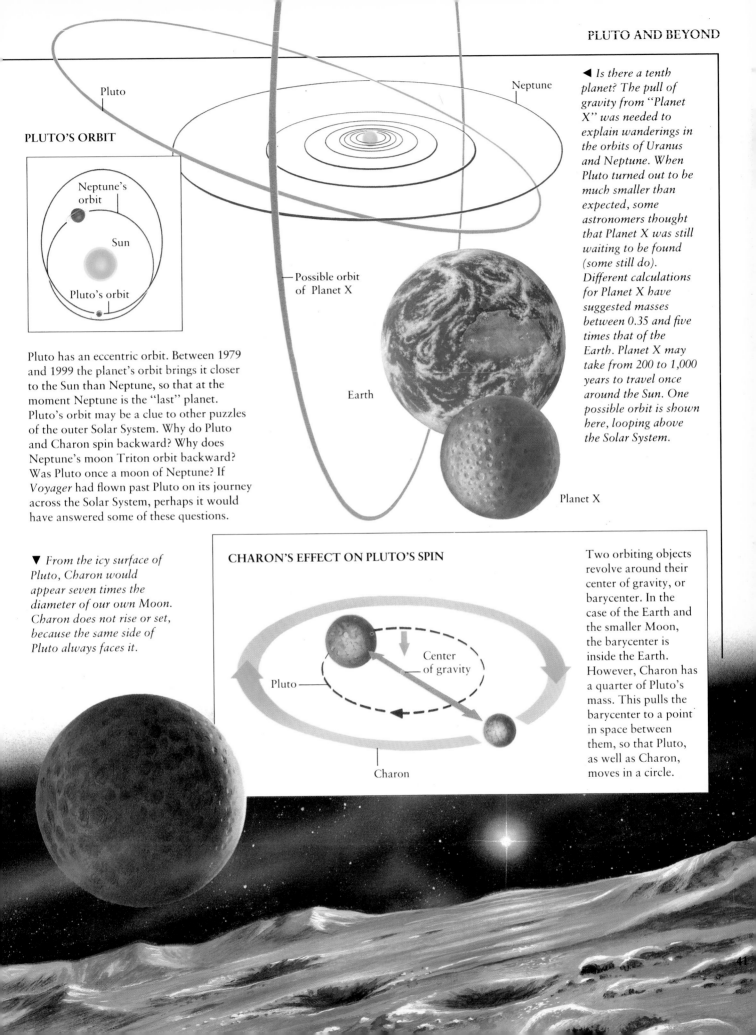

Neptune's orbit

Sun

Pluto's orbit

Pluto

Neptune

Possible orbit of Planet X

Earth

Planet X

Pluto has an eccentric orbit. Between 1979 and 1999 the planet's orbit brings it closer to the Sun than Neptune, so that at the moment Neptune is the "last" planet. Pluto's orbit may be a clue to other puzzles of the outer Solar System. Why do Pluto and Charon spin backward? Why does Neptune's moon Triton orbit backward? Was Pluto once a moon of Neptune? If *Voyager* had flown past Pluto on its journey across the Solar System, perhaps it would have answered some of these questions.

◄ *Is there a tenth planet? The pull of gravity from "Planet X" was needed to explain wanderings in the orbits of Uranus and Neptune. When Pluto turned out to be much smaller than expected, some astronomers thought that Planet X was still waiting to be found (some still do). Different calculations for Planet X have suggested masses between 0.35 and five times that of the Earth. Planet X may take from 200 to 1,000 years to travel once around the Sun. One possible orbit is shown here, looping above the Solar System.*

▼ *From the icy surface of Pluto, Charon would appear seven times the diameter of our own Moon. Charon does not rise or set, because the same side of Pluto always faces it.*

CHARON'S EFFECT ON PLUTO'S SPIN

Center of gravity

Pluto

Charon

Two orbiting objects revolve around their center of gravity, or barycenter. In the case of the Earth and the smaller Moon, the barycenter is inside the Earth. However, Charon has a quarter of Pluto's mass. This pulls the barycenter to a point in space between them, so that Pluto, as well as Charon, moves in a circle.

Minor Planets and Meteoroids

In the early days of the Solar System there was debris everywhere, as grains of solid matter grew together into larger objects. The planets and the larger satellites were the most successful, but countless other smaller bodies formed as well. Some passed too near a planet, especially Jupiter, whose gravity kept them from growing into major planets. Other bodies, moving in the wide space between the orbits of Mars and Jupiter, collided and broke up. The remains of these are known as asteroids, or minor planets.

FACTS ABOUT THE MINOR PLANETS

• Ceres was the first asteroid, or minor planet, to be discovered, in 1801.
• Some asteroids have orbits that take them very close to Earth. One, called Hermes, has come within 483,000 mi. (777,000 km) of us. However, the threat of an asteroid colliding with Earth is very small.

▶ *The asteroid belt is found between the orbits of Mars and Jupiter. It probably contains about 100,000 bodies larger than 0.6 mi. (1 km) across. Over 3,000 of the largest have been given names. The largest, Ceres, has a diameter of 620 mi. (1,000 km). Asteroid 1991 DA travels well past Jupiter. The asteroids known as the Trojans share Jupiter's orbit. At its closest point to the Sun the asteroid Phaethon glows red-hot, as it passes twice as close to the Sun as the planet Mercury. The orbits of some other unusual asteroids are shown here.*

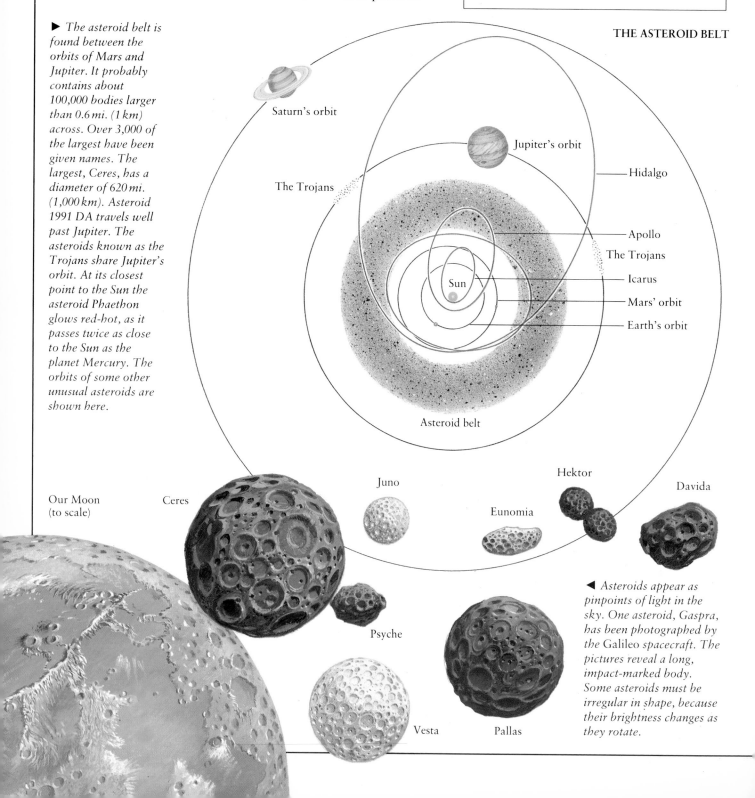

THE ASTEROID BELT

Saturn's orbit

Jupiter's orbit

The Trojans

Hidalgo

Apollo

The Trojans

Icarus

Mars' orbit

Earth's orbit

Sun

Asteroid belt

Our Moon (to scale)

Ceres

Juno

Eunomia

Hektor

Davida

Psyche

Vesta

Pallas

◀ *Asteroids appear as pinpoints of light in the sky. One asteroid, Gaspra, has been photographed by the Galileo spacecraft. The pictures reveal a long, impact-marked body. Some asteroids must be irregular in shape, because their brightness changes as they rotate.*

◀ *An especially bright meteor is called a fireball. Any meteor large enough to travel through the Earth's atmosphere and hit the ground is called a meteorite. These are thought to be pieces of minor planets or comets. Some meteorites are stony, others are metallic—presumably from the crust or core of a broken mini-planet. A few meteorites are made of very crumbly rock.*

METEOROIDS

Many meteoroids are particles thrown out from the crumbly nucleus of a comet *(see pages 44–45)*. They exist by the million, traveling along the comet's orbit in huge swarms, though the grains may be miles apart. Meteoroids themselves are invisible, but if they collide with the Earth's atmosphere (at speeds from 6 to 25 mi/s. [10 to 40 km/s]) they evaporate in a streak of light—forming meteors, or "shooting stars."

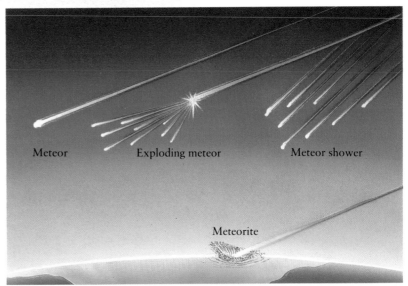

Meteor   Exploding meteor   Meteor shower

Meteorite

▼ *If the Earth passes through a large swarm of meteoroids, many meteors may be seen every hour. This is a meteor shower. The meteor shower below is connected with the comet Tempel-Tuttle.*

▶ *Ordinary meteors usually burn up at about 30 mi. (50 km) above the Earth. Anything larger than a small stone will light up the sky as a fireball. It may explode, or hit the ground as a meteorite.*

▼ *The Old Woman meteorite was discovered in California in 1976. It weighs 6,080 lb. (2,758 kg)—the second largest meteorite ever found in the United States. It is made of iron and nickel and may once have formed part of the molten core of a small planet that broke up about 4 billion years ago.*

Comets

It is easy to understand how the unexpected sight of a comet's long, bright tail in the sky must have terrified ancient civilizations. Today we know that comets are just lumps of ice and rock, traveling from the far outer Solar System to orbit our Sun. As a comet nears the Sun the ice melts, giving off jets of gas and releasing clouds of dusty rock particles. From the Earth this gas and dust is seen as a dramatic tail, shining by reflected sunlight, and stretching for millions of miles.

Crumbling particles of rock and ice

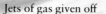 Nucleus

Jets of gas given off

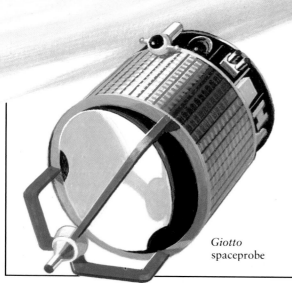

Giotto spaceprobe

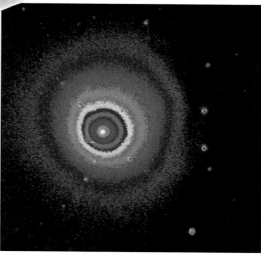

▲ Comets are named after the person who discovers them. Comet West, discovered by Richard West in 1976, was one of the brightest of recent times.

◀ The solid part of a comet, called its nucleus, may be only a couple of miles across, but it may produce a coma, or cloud, of dust and gas, 10 times the Earth's diameter. (Illustration not to scale.)

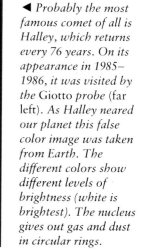

◀ Probably the most famous comet of all is Halley, which returns every 76 years. On its appearance in 1985–1986, it was visited by the Giotto probe (far left). As Halley neared our planet this false color image was taken from Earth. The different colors show different levels of brightness (white is brightest). The nucleus gives out gas and dust in circular rings.

Tail shrinks

◀ *As a comet nears the Sun, gas sent out from its nucleus is forced away from the Sun by the solar wind. Dust particles are pushed back by the pressure of the Sun's radiation on them, and they form a separate tail. The closer the comet comes to the Sun, the faster the gas and dust are released. At Halley's nearest point to the Sun, about 14 tons of its ice was turning into gas every second.*

▲ *Halley's Comet appeared over Jerusalem in A.D. 66. The first recorded sighting of Halley's Comet dates from 240 B.C.*

Orbit of a comet

Tail develops

Sun

Tail builds up

Earth

Dust tail

Earth's orbit

Gas tail

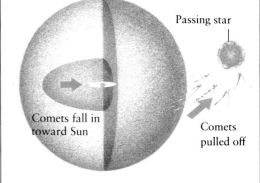

Passing star

Comets fall in toward Sun

Comets pulled off

WHERE ARE COMETS FROM?
No one knows for sure where comets come from. One suggestion is that they may form a vast cloud surrounding the Solar System. The gravitational effect of passing stars pulls comets from the cloud to fall finally toward the Sun and shine briefly in the sky.

FACTS ABOUT COMETS

● Some comets take thousands of years to go around the Sun once, but Comet Encke takes just over three years.
● Comet Biela was first seen in 1806. When it returned in 1845, it divided into two comets.
● The comet Schwassmann-Wachmann orbits the Sun almost in a circle. It revolves beyond Mars and can always be seen.
● In 1983 the comet IRAS-Araki-Alcock passed within 3 million mi. (5 million km) of the Earth— the closest a comet has come since 1770.

● Comet Ikeya-Seki, which was first seen in 1965, is said to be a Sun-grazer, passing the Sun about 40 times closer than Mercury.
● Halley's Comet was named after Edmund Halley (1656–1742), an English scientist. Halley believed that comets seen in 1531, 1607 and 1682 were in fact the same comet. He suggested that this comet would return in 1758. His prediction was proved right on Christmas Day 1758. Halley's discovery was important proof that the law of gravity worked for comets.

▶ *The time a comet takes to complete its orbit around the Sun is known as its period. Short-period comets take from a few years to several decades to orbit the Sun. A long-period comet may take thousands of years to return again. Some short-period orbits are shown* right.

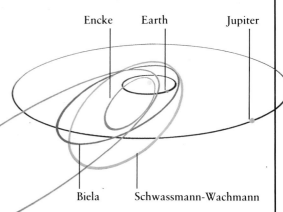

Encke   Earth   Jupiter

Halley

Biela   Schwassmann-Wachmann

BEYOND THE SOLAR SYSTEM

The Milky Way

The Sun is just one of a hundred billion stars, existing in space in a vast "star-city." This city is our galaxy, which we call the Milky Way. The softly-shining band of light in our night sky is also called the Milky Way, and is the edge-on view of our own galaxy. The Milky Way is spiral in shape, and the Sun is found out toward its "edge." The galaxy is so huge that it would take a beam of light about 100,000 years to cross from one edge to the other, even though light travels at almost 186,000 mi. (300,000 km) a second. Huge areas of the Milky Way are unexplored because our view of them is so poor—it is like trying to see people at the other side of a crowd. Dark clouds block the light from the center of the galaxy, increasing the astronomers' problems. However, observing other galaxies has helped to build up a picture of what our own is like.

THE MILKY WAY
The Milky Way is a barred spiral galaxy, with two arms that rotate slowly. The area in which our Sun is found takes about 225 million years to go around once. At the center is a bright halo of old stars that formed with the galaxy, 14 billion years ago. The arms contain vast nebulae of gas and dust where new stars are being born.

HOW A GALAXY BEGINS
Galaxies begin as huge masses of dark gas. As they shrink under the pressure of gravity (1), the gas at the center becomes dense enough to start forming stars. Some galaxies start spinning (2), and if the spin is fast enough it forces the outer areas into a flat disk, forming a spiral (3) or barred spiral galaxy. Galaxies that spin slowly or not at all become spherical or elliptical in shape.

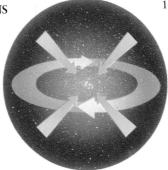

1

▲ A slowly-spinning mass of gas starts to collapse, and the first stars are formed at the center. As the cloud shrinks, its turning speed increases.

2

▲ Gas clouds meet in the swirling disk, and attract more clouds because of their extra gravity. Stars start to form here too.

3

▲ There is no gas left at the center to make new stars, but the arms are rich in raw star material. The galaxy is now in its prime of life.

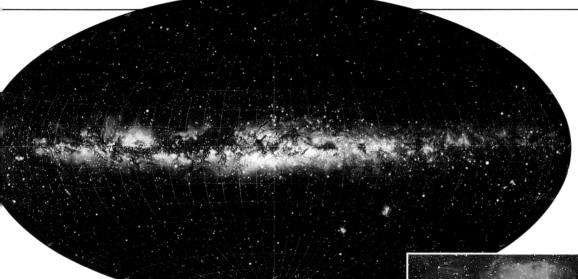

◄ *This panorama of our galaxy was obtained by combining several photographs taken of the Milky Way from different parts of the world. If you imagine the right and left ends joined together, with your head inside the ring, this is how the Milky Way would appear to someone floating in space.*

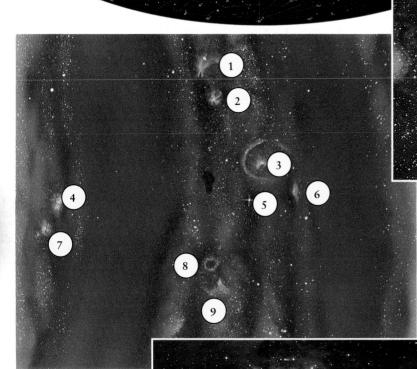

▼ *The Orion Nebula is about 30 light-years across and 1,600 light-years away. It was once dark, but millions of years ago stars began forming inside it, and their radiation makes the nebula glow.*

▲ *The Milky Way is rich in dark nebulae. However, the galaxy is foggy with tiny particles that act as a color filter. The effect causes objects like this nebula to appear red to us on Earth.*

▲ *Within the main arms of the Milky Way are smaller arms where stars and nebulae are more closely connected. This illustration shows some of the Sun's neighbors in the galaxy.*

1 Cone Nebula
2 Rosette Nebula
3 Orion Nebula
4 Lagoon Nebula
5 Solar System
6 California Nebula
7 Trifid Nebula
8 Vela Supernova Remnant
9 N. American Nebula

MILKY WAY DATAFILE

Diameter:
    130,000 light-years
Thickness of spiral arms:
    3,000 light-years (approx.)
Thickness of central bulge:
    10,000 light-years
Diameter of central bulge:
    20,000 light-years
Total mass: 110 billion × Sun
Average density (estimate):
    0.00000000000000000007
    (water = 1)
Age: 14 billion years
Time to rotate once:
    (Position of Sun)
    225 million years
Distance of Sun from center:
    30,000 light-years
Satellite galaxies: 2

Clusters and Superclusters

Just as stars are born in groups or clusters, so do galaxies often exist in groups. Our galaxy belongs to a cluster of some 32 galaxies, called the Local Group. Most of the galaxies in the Local Group are small and faint and would be invisible to us if they were much farther away. Beyond the edge of the Local Group, astronomers have discovered thousands of other groups of galaxies in the universe. These groups in turn seem to form looser groups in space, known as superclusters.

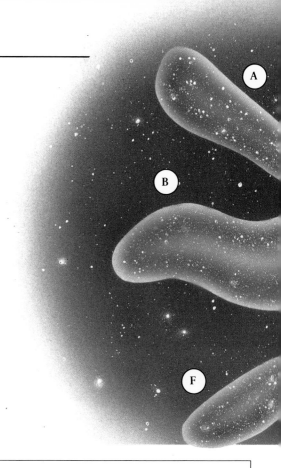

TYPES OF GALAXY

◄ *Galaxies are put into classes according to their shape. Irregular galaxies (class Irr) are usually smaller than the Milky Way. The gravity of much larger galaxies nearby may have pulled them out of shape—for example, the Magellanic Clouds, in the grip of the Milky Way.*

▶ *Elliptical galaxies seem to have no nebulae, which means they cannot form any more stars. They are scaled from E0 (almost spherical) to E7 (very elongated). The largest known galaxies are giant ellipticals, but dwarf ellipticals are also very common.*

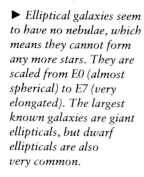

◄ *Ordinary spiral galaxies are classed from Sa (very tight arms) to Sc (very loose arms). Another type, S0, has a very large nucleus, or center, which is more like an elliptical galaxy's. Until very recently the Milky Way galaxy was thought to be an Sb or Sc type.*

▶ *Barred spiral galaxies, classed from SBa (tight arms) to SBc (loose arms), have centers with a short bar of stars across them. The spiral arms begin at the ends of this bar. Astronomers have recently found evidence that there is such a bar in our own Milky Way galaxy.*

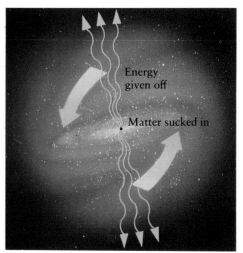

Energy given off

Matter sucked in

QUASARS

The strangest galaxies known are the far-off objects called quasars. Although they cannot be seen in any detail, they seem to be galaxies that are sending out huge amounts of energy from a small area of space near their center. Some quasars are as bright as thousands of galaxies like the Milky Way. The source of this energy could be the presence of a black hole at the galaxy's center, which is sucking gas and whole stars into it (*see pages 56–57*). As it is sucked in, this material spins around the black hole almost at the speed of light, sending huge amounts of energy into space.

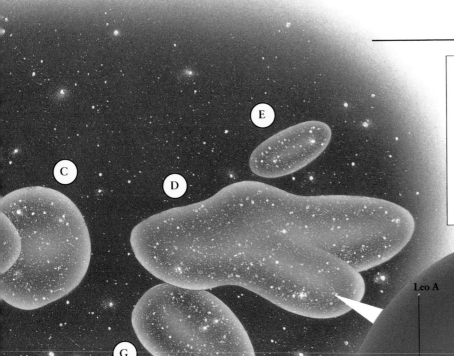

◀ *The Local Supercluster contains several thousand galaxies, scattered across 100 million light-years of space. The Milky Way galaxy is near the outer edge of the Canes Venatici cloud.*

KEY
A Virgo III cloud
B Virgo II cloud
C Virgo I cloud
D Canes Venatici cloud
E Canes Venatici spur
F Crater cloud
G Leo II cloud

SUPERCLUSTERS

The Local Group is a fairly small cluster of galaxies, belonging to a collection of other small clusters called the Canes Venatici cloud. A much larger group of galaxies, the Virgo cluster, is about 60 million light-years away. It lies at the center of our Local Supercluster—a collection of major clouds of galaxies. The entire supercluster measures over 100 million light-years across. In the diagram *(above)*, the galaxy clusters are shown with sharp boundaries to help make their shapes more clear. In reality, the clusters are much more scattered throughout space. Notice how the central Virgo I cloud is round, while the others are elongated, pointing inward toward Virgo I as if stretched by the pull of its gravity. This has occurred because Virgo I, although not particularly large, contains about 20 percent of all the galaxies in the supercluster.

▲ *The 32 galaxies detected in our Local Group range from the Andromeda galaxy, the largest, to tiny irregular galaxies. The Milky Way is second in order of size, one of only three spiral galaxies in the Group. The galaxies can be pictured scattered in space, inside an imaginary sphere about 5 million light-years across.*

FACTS ABOUT THE LOCAL GROUP

• The Andromeda galaxy is the largest in the Local Group. It may contain 400 billion stars.
• The Milky Way's nearest neighbors in space are the two Magellanic Clouds, 200,000 light-years away. They are satellites of the Milky Way.
• A belt of fast-moving gas, called the Magellanic Stream, connects our galaxy to the two Magellanic Clouds.

• M33 in Triangulum is the third-largest member of the Local Group.
• The most distant galaxy in our Local Group is Leo A, 5 million light-years away.
• Dwarf elliptical galaxies are probably the commonest type of galaxy in the Universe, but they are so dim that we can only make out the 15 or so near to us in the Local Group.

▶ *A supernova, or exploding star, plays an important part in a galaxy's development. Such stars scatter extra elements into space, besides the original hydrogen and helium, to build up new stars. The last nearby supernova was seen in the Large Magellanic Cloud in 1987.*

Cosmology

Cosmology is the study of how the universe began and how it will be in the future. The universe may go on getting bigger forever. Alternatively, the galaxies may come together, until finally they collide and explode in the violence of a "Big Crunch." Cosmologists try to work out the likely fate of the universe. They believe they have traced the development of the universe back to a fraction of a second after the Big Bang, but they do not know what caused the Big Bang itself.

THE FATE OF THE UNIVERSE

What is the future of the universe? It may keep on expanding; it may collapse and end; or it may even be one of a series of universes. It all depends upon how much material the universe contains. As the galaxies fly apart after the Big Bang, their gravitational attraction is slowing them down. But the gravity between bodies in space becomes weaker as they move farther apart, so the slowing-down effect becomes less as the universe expands. There is a thin dividing line between there not being enough matter in the universe—so that gravity is too weak ever to stop the expansion—and there being too much matter—so that everything rushes together in a "Big Crunch."

AN EVER-EXPANDING UNIVERSE

Big Bang

Galaxies fly apart
after the Big Bang

A FINITE UNIVERSE

Big Bang

FACTS ABOUT THE UNIVERSE

• There are clues to show that the Big Bang occurred. For one thing, the galaxies are still flying apart from the explosion. In 1965 astronomers found a very feeble warmth in space, which is a trace of the fantastic heat created by the Big Bang.

• Some astronomers believe the universe must contain "missing mass." This is invisible material that astronomers believe exists because of the effect of its gravity. If the universe does not contain this material, then after the Big Bang it should have expanded so fast that galaxies could not have formed at all. The missing mass has not been detected yet, but it may add up to roughly ten times the mass of the stars and nebulae that are visible.

RED SHIFT

Light travels in waves, and the color of light depends upon wavelength. Waves of blue light are much closer together than waves of red light. If a very fast-moving object is sending out light, the light waves will be squashed ahead of it and stretched out behind. This means that the light from the approaching object seems bluish. Light from an object traveling fast away from someone appears reddish. This is called a red shift.

Reddish light
detected on
Earth

Galaxy moving
away from Earth

◀ *Distant galaxies show a color shift toward red. These galaxies are moving away at speeds of thousands of miles a second. Their light waves are stretched by this speed, making them look redder in color than they really are. This change of color is not seen by the eye, but is detected with an instrument called a spectrograph. Astronomers can use the red shift to measure the speed at which a galaxy travels.*

▼ *Galaxies and clusters of galaxies twist and loop themselves through space like strings of frog spawn (eggs). Is there almost as much invisible matter in the supposedly empty space between the strings?*

Gravity cannot stop the expansion of the universe

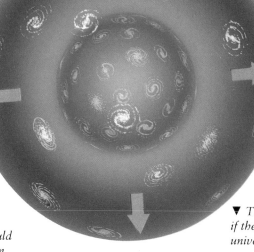

Gravity stops expansion of the universe

▼ *If the Big Crunch occurred, the sky would grow as hot as the Sun. Finally, everything would vanish into a black hole.*

A SERIES OF UNIVERSES
A completely new universe begins

▼ *Time and space would end if the universe ended. A new universe would have to start everything again. It would not be the old one recycled.*

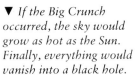

Big Crunch   Big Bang

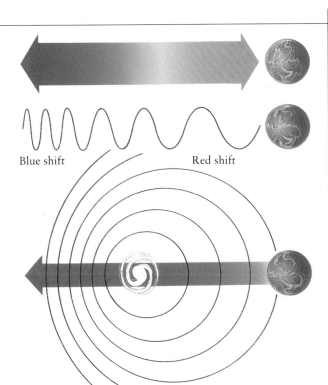

Blue shift   Red shift

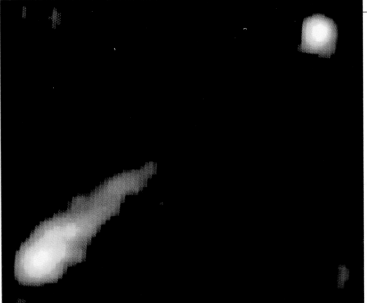

▲ *Red shift measurements of the quasar 3C 273 show that it is 2.1 billion light-years away, traveling 30,000 mi./s (50,000 km/s). As the universe expands, distant galaxies move away faster than galaxies nearby. Their distance can be calculated from their red shift.*

THE STARS

The Life of a Star

A star is born inside a huge nebula of gas and dust (called "gust"). A nebula starts to shrink into much smaller nebulae when it receives a "shake," perhaps after colliding with another nebula, or being hit by the shock waves of an exploding star. Eventually the nebula will break up into a cluster of baby stars, containing a mixture of bright, medium, and dim stars. Although all these stars are born at the same time, their lifetimes and endings will be very different, according to the amount of material they contain. Generally, a massive star has a shorter life than a less massive star. Stars are sources of light and heat. They also process and recycle material, turning some of the hydrogen and helium that were created at the beginning of the universe into other elements. These include carbon and oxygen, which are the building blocks of life.

► *A medium-hot star, like the Sun, gives out much less energy than the brightest stars. This means it will shine steadily for billions of years before it begins to expand. The dimmer the star, the longer its life.*

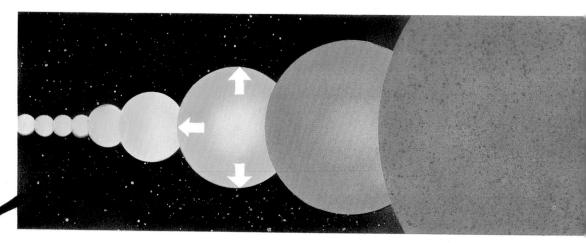

▲ *The main sequence period for both a medium-hot star and a very hot, bright star (below) is the time when the star is shining steadily by turning hydrogen into helium. The star grows slightly hotter and brighter during this time. When the star's core of used helium reaches a certain size it is a crisis point in its life. The core of the star collapses under the force of its gravity and becomes still hotter. Now even helium starts nuclear reactions.*

▲ *This new energy source is so powerful that part of the star is blown outward. The outer layers cool to a reddish color. At this stage in its life the star is known as a "red giant." At its greatest size, the diameter of a red giant may be a hundred times that of the original star, which forms the core of the red giant.*

► *A very bright, very hot star may shine at full power for only a few million years before it uses up all its fuel. Although it has more fuel than a medium star, it uses it up much faster, and has only a brief life.*

Blue
giant

Red
dwarf

Main sequence star
(such as the Sun)

Red giant

White
dwarf

Neutron
star

Black hole

▲ *Although our Sun shines with a yellowish light, not all stars are yellow. Stars vary in size, brightness, and temperature. The hottest stars shine with a white-blue light; they have a diameter up to 20 times greater than our Sun, and so are known as blue giants. The dim, cool stars known as red dwarfs are about a quarter of the Sun's diameter. Huge red giant stars have outer layers that have blown away from the core of energy, becoming cooler and so redder. They can be 500 times the Sun's width. A dim white dwarf will give out little light and may be only a few percent of the Sun's width.*

◀ *In a white dwarf, the star's atoms are crushed together hundreds of times more tightly than normal. A neutron star is a dead star, made from the solid nuclei of atoms, the densest material in the universe. If it is massive enough, a neutron star will become a black hole.*

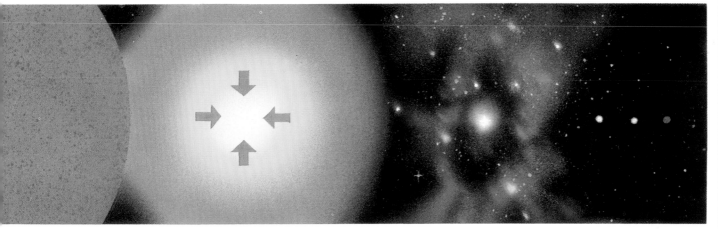

▲ *Eventually the core runs out of fuel and collapses completely, because it is no longer producing enough energy to balance the shrinking force of gravity. This is the end of nuclear reactions in the star's core. If the star is much more massive than our Sun, its collapse gives out so much energy that the star is blown to pieces in a supernova explosion (below).*

▲ *The collapse of a star like the Sun will not result in a dramatic supernova explosion. Instead, the star will shrink to a hot body the size of a small planet. The star is now called a white dwarf. The gravity of a massive star, however, will be so strong it will crush the nuclei of the star's atoms together, making a tiny, very dense, neutron star (below).*

▲ *An ordinary star, after becoming a white dwarf, cools into a dead black dwarf.*

▼ *If a neutron star has a mass greater than five Suns it will form a black hole.*

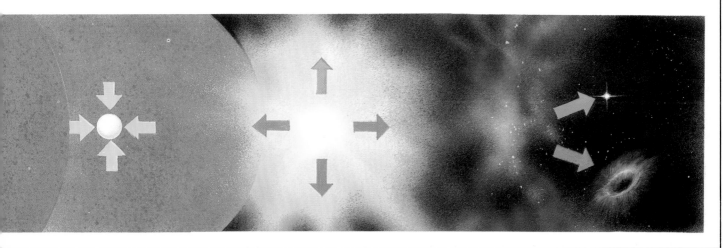

Extraordinary Stars

If you think of a star as a body similar to our Sun, the different stars shown here may surprise you. Not all stars shine at constant levels. Some, known as variable stars, change greatly in brightness during years or even days. Other stars, called pulsars, spin faster than a washing machine. Twenty percent of all known stars have a partner, around which they orbit in a binary (two-part) system. Occasionally the transfer of gas in a binary system can lead to the drama of a supernova, or exploding star.

VARIABLE STARS

A variable star may be an unstable star that goes through a stage when it starts to swell and shrink, changing its brightness. Other variable stars may occur in binary systems where gas passes from one star to another, causing a sudden flare. A few variable stars do not actually give out less light at all, but seem to do so because they orbit each other in a binary system, and the light from one star is blocked for a time by its "partner."

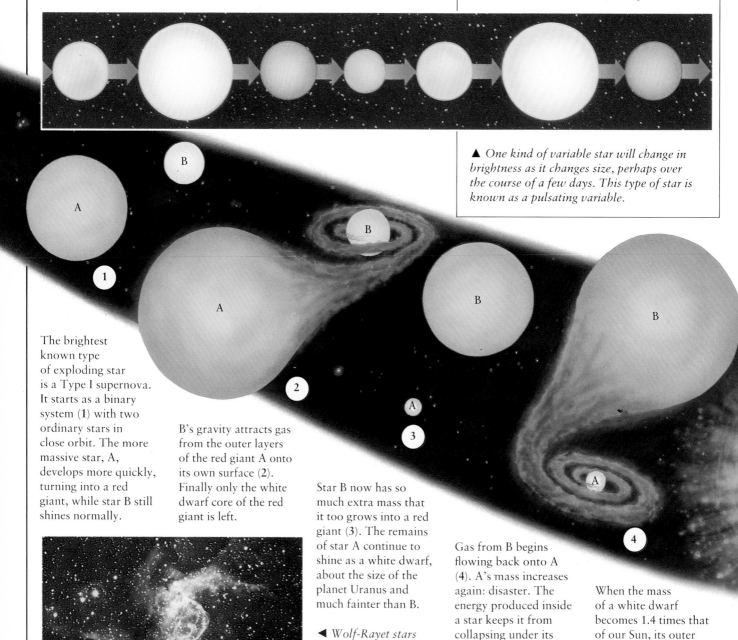

▲ One kind of variable star will change in brightness as it changes size, perhaps over the course of a few days. This type of star is known as a pulsating variable.

The brightest known type of exploding star is a Type I supernova. It starts as a binary system (**1**) with two ordinary stars in close orbit. The more massive star, A, develops more quickly, turning into a red giant, while star B still shines normally.

B's gravity attracts gas from the outer layers of the red giant A onto its own surface (**2**). Finally only the white dwarf core of the red giant is left.

Star B now has so much extra mass that it too grows into a red giant (**3**). The remains of star A continue to shine as a white dwarf, about the size of the planet Uranus and much fainter than B.

◄ Wolf-Rayet stars are the hottest stars known. The one at the center of this nebula has a surface temperature of about 90,000°F (50,000°C).

Gas from B begins flowing back onto A (**4**). A's mass increases again: disaster. The energy produced inside a star keeps it from collapsing under its own weight. However, a white dwarf has used up most of its nuclear fuel. If too much mass is added, A won't be able to hold its shape.

When the mass of a white dwarf becomes 1.4 times that of our Sun, its outer layers fall in with such force that the temperature rises to several billion degrees. The blast of energy blows the star apart (**5**).

PULSAR

In 1967, radio astronomers at Cambridge, England, were trying out a new telescope. It began to record bursts of radiation that repeated every couple of seconds. At first the Cambridge astronomers thought that this might be an intelligent message from space, but soon they realized that they had discovered a new kind of star—a pulsar. From that chance discovery, more than 400 radio pulsars were discovered in the next 20 years.

▶ *A pulsar is a rapidly spinning neutron star. Its fierce magnetic field squirts light and radio waves into beams of energy that sweep around as the star turns. If the beam crosses Earth the star is detected by the pulse of its radiation.*

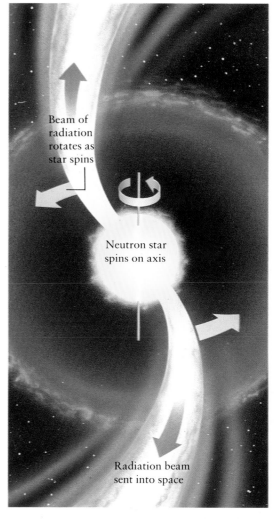

Beam of radiation rotates as star spins

Neutron star spins on axis

Radiation beam sent into space

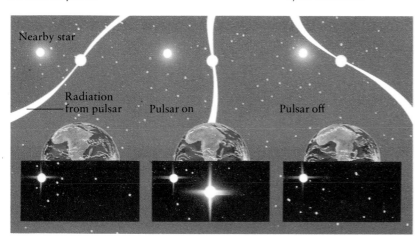

Nearby star

Radiation from pulsar

Pulsar on

Pulsar off

▲ *Pulsars flash on and off when their radiation beam passes across the Earth. Even the slowest pulsar sends out one pulse every four seconds. The most rapid one spins 622 times a second. Why do neutron stars spin so much faster than the original star? Find the answer by watching an ice skater spin on the ice. As the skater shrinks by folding her arms up close to her body, she speeds up. A star collapsing into a tiny neutron star has the same effect.*

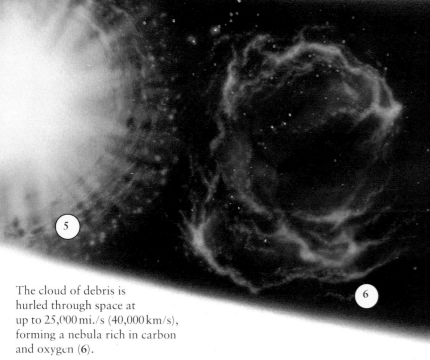

The cloud of debris is hurled through space at up to 25,000 mi./s (40,000 km/s), forming a nebula rich in carbon and oxygen (**6**).

BINARY STARS

In some binary systems the two stars (**1**) may be very close, orbiting each other in a few hours; in others, the stars are millions of miles apart. Often, one star is more massive than the other and has evolved, perhaps into a red giant (**2**). Although the stars in a binary system appear to revolve around each other, they are really moving around their common centers of gravity (**3**).

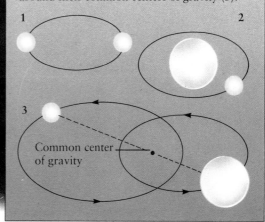

Common center of gravity

Black Holes and Neutron Stars

When a massive star dies, it may leave behind a heavy core which becomes a neutron star—the smallest, densest kind of star. If the force of gravity around the neutron star is strong enough, a black hole could be the result. These fascinating objects occur when gravity is so strong that space acts like a one-way funnel. Anything—light rays or moving solid matter—that passes into this funnel is compressed to nothing and disappears from our universe. A black hole is the end of space and time.

▶ *A binary system containing a black hole will be ablaze with radiation, because material from the other star is energized as it spirals into the black hole.*

WHAT IS A BLACK HOLE LIKE?

A black hole is caused by a very dense object, such as a massive neutron star, which creates a powerful gravitational field—a kind of space funnel—in a small space. An object passing close enough will be pulled into the space funnel; once something has been pulled into a black hole it can never escape.

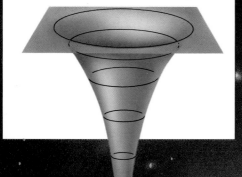

▲ *A black hole on its own in space would be difficult to detect. But if it is near another star, the pull of the black hole's gravity may draw material from the star into a whirling ring that gives off bursts of X-rays. If astronomers detect a starlike object that is giving out high-energy radiation they have probably found a black hole.*

A BLACK HOLE IN THE MILKY WAY?

A faint object in the Milky Way galaxy, normally about a million times too faint to be seen with the naked eye, sometimes gives out bursts of X-rays. Known as V404 Cygni, it is the most likely black hole in our galaxy. V404 Cygni is a binary system. The two stars orbit each other in 6.5 days. One star may be similar to the Sun, the other is a very dense object about six times as massive as the Sun—as massive as a black hole should be.

NEUTRON STARS

All objects in the Universe are made of atoms, and atoms consist of atomic particles in rapid motion. The forces holding an atom in shape are very powerful. But even they can be broken. When a star runs out of nuclear fuel and collapses, the pressure at the center can be so enormous that the atoms themselves are compressed into a tiny ball of solid neutrons (consisting of protons and electrons forced together), millions of times smaller and denser than the atoms in the original star.

▼ *In order to collapse into a neutron star, a star must have a mass about 1.4 times the Sun's mass. This is called the mass limit. Such a star would be over a hundred times the Earth's size, but it would shrink into a neutron star 12 mi. (20 km) across—the size of a large city.*

▲ *If the Earth were compressed into solid neutrons, it would be a ball the diameter of a large sports field. A marble made of solid neutrons would weigh about as much as a thousand fully laden battleships.*

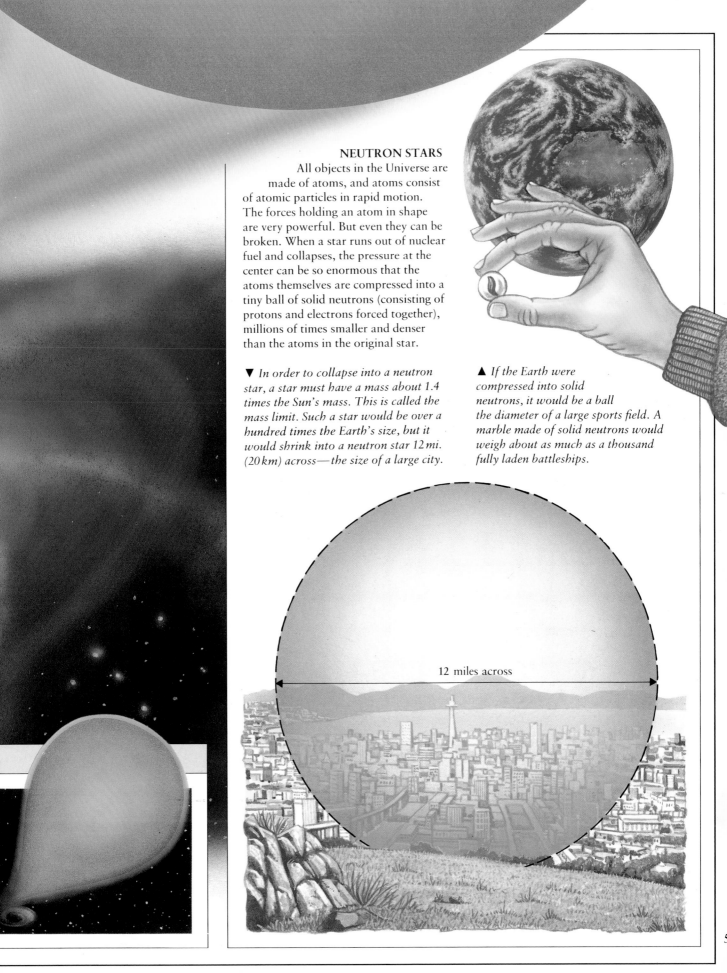

12 miles across

Star Distance, Star Brightness

To measure the distance of a star from Earth, astronomers use parallax (*see opposite*). The first star distance was measured in 1838, marking a milestone in astronomy. As more star distances were cataloged, astronomers realized that some nearby stars appeared fainter than more distant ones, instead of the other way around as expected. It was proof that stars had different brightnesses, or luminosities. This formed the basis for the classification of stars into the families that are recognized today.

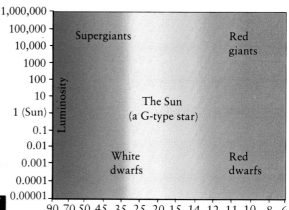

◄ *A group of stars close together in the sky is known as a star cluster. Clusters such as the Pleiades (left) are very useful for astronomers, because the stars are all the same distance away from Earth. So if one star looks brighter than another, it must be more luminous by that amount. The Pleiades are very young, maybe a hundred million years old, and the brightest members are very hot main sequence stars.*

▲ *The Hertzsprung-Russell Diagram plots the temperature and luminosity of stars. Generally, the more material a star has, the hotter it is. A blue giant star is found in the upper left of the diagram. The Sun, a yellow star of average size, lies in the middle, or main sequence. Few stars do not belong to the main sequence. Red giant stars lie in the upper right of the diagram. Lower left stars are white dwarfs —very hot, but dim.*

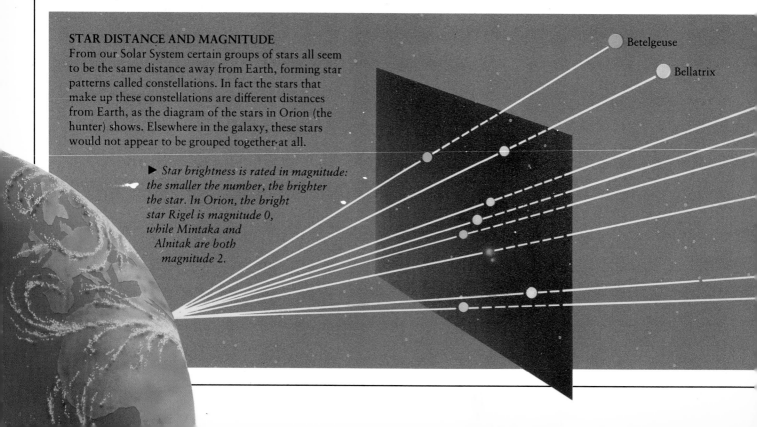

STAR DISTANCE AND MAGNITUDE
From our Solar System certain groups of stars all seem to be the same distance away from Earth, forming star patterns called constellations. In fact the stars that make up these constellations are different distances from Earth, as the diagram of the stars in Orion (the hunter) shows. Elsewhere in the galaxy, these stars would not appear to be grouped together at all.

► *Star brightness is rated in magnitude: the smaller the number, the brighter the star. In Orion, the bright star Rigel is magnitude 0, while Mintaka and Alnitak are both magnitude 2.*

PARALLAX

When you move your head from side to side, nearby objects seem to move more than distant ones. This is called parallax. Astronomers use parallax to find out how far away stars are from Earth. They take two measurements of the direction of a star about six months apart, when the Earth is on opposite sides of its orbit and has moved 186 million mi. (300 million km) through space. From the slight change in the star's position, its distance can be calculated. The farther the star, the smaller the change.

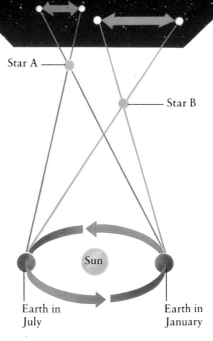

Star A

Star B

Sun

Earth in July

Earth in January

◀ *A very hot star will look bluish-white, and a cooler one, yellow. Stars may be classified according to temperature (far left). Letters stand for different temperature bands. Our yellow Sun is a G star. The table (left) shows the luminosity of average stars in these classes.*

	W
	O B
	A
	F
	G
	K
	M
	R
	N S

	−1
	0
	1
	2
	3
	4
	5
	6
	7

FACTS ABOUT STARS

● The nearest star to our Sun is Proxima Centauri, 4.2 light-years away. It is a dim red dwarf star.
● Sirius is the brightest star in our sky.
● The dimmest stars we are able to detect from Earth are about 1×10^{27} times fainter than the dimmest star visible with the naked eye.
● The oldest known star is thought to be CS 22876 − 32. It may be 15 billion years old.
● There are many newborn stars visible. An example is L1551, which is being born now in a nebula 500 light-years away.
● Pulsar PSR 1957 + 20 is the fastest spinning star. It revolves 622 times a second.
● The supernova seen in A.D. 1006 appeared about 40 times brighter than Venus.

Mintaka

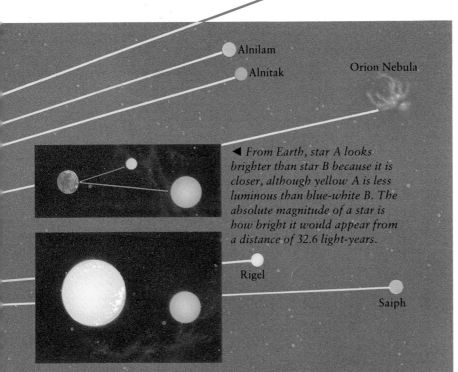

Alnilam

Alnitak

Orion Nebula

◀ *From Earth, star A looks brighter than star B because it is closer, although yellow A is less luminous than blue-white B. The absolute magnitude of a star is how bright it would appear from a distance of 32.6 light-years.*

Rigel

Saiph

▲ *From Earth, all the stars of Orion seem to be the same distance away, forming a particular pattern in our night sky. But Betelgeuse is 330 light-years from Earth, and Mintaka is 2,300 light-years away.*

The Moving Sky

To an observer on Earth, the stars appear to be attached to the inside of a vast hollow globe which spins around the Earth from east to west once a day. This view is not true. It is the Earth, and not the sky, that is spinning. All the same, it is often useful for astronomers to pretend that this celestial sphere, or globe, in the sky really does exist. The Earth's poles, and lines of latitude and longitude, can then all be marked on the celestial sphere. This helps astronomers to map the position of stars in the sky.

FURTHER FACTS

Homing pigeons use the Sun and stars to find their way. Experiments in planetariums have shown that the pigeons recognize certain stars or star patterns, but the Sun and stars appear in different parts of the sky at different times, so they must also have a built-in "clock" to allow for this effect.

▶ *The celestial sphere appears to spin around the north and south celestial poles, which line up with the Earth's axis. It is divided up into 24 segments, running from the north to the south pole. In an hour it turns through one of these segments, carrying the stars steadily around the sky. The stars form easily recognizable patterns in the night sky. These patterns are called constellations. They are always in the same place on the celestial sphere, so their position can be noted. Astronomers can use the constellations to know where to find a particular star.*

▶ *The celestial equator is a projected circle, in line with the Earth's equator. To an observer standing on the Equator, stars lying near the celestial equator pass overhead.*

North celestial pole

Constellation

Celestial equator

South celestial pole

FACTS ABOUT THE MOVING SKY

• An observer always has part of the celestial sphere blocked out by the Earth. For example, the famous constellation Crux (the Cross), which lies near the south celestial pole, cannot be seen from Europe or from much of North America.
• Different constellations are seen from Earth in summer and winter. For example, in Europe, Orion is high in the midnight sky in January but cannot be seen in July at all. This is because the Earth's movement has positioned the Sun between it and Orion. The best time to look for a particular star is during the time of year when it is on the opposite side of the Earth to the Sun.

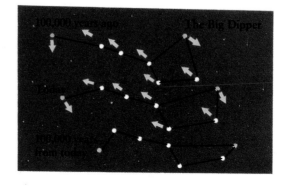

100,000 years ago   The Big Dipper

Today

100,000 years from today

◀ *The stars are moving through space at great speed, which means the star patterns are changing very slowly. The Big Dipper in Ursa Major is an example. Five stars in this group are moving one way, and two the opposite way.*

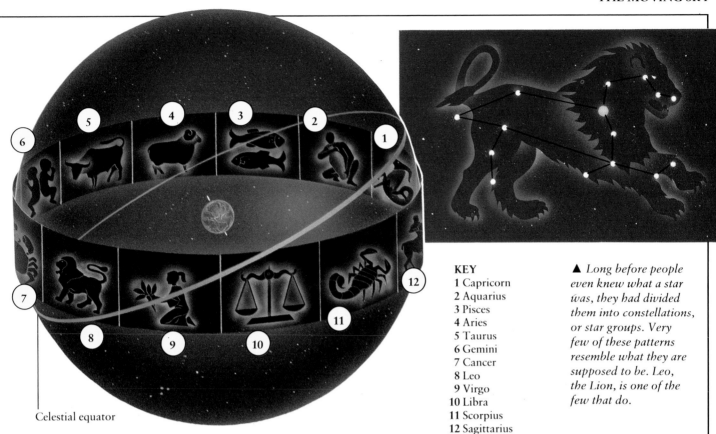

Celestial equator

KEY
1 Capricorn
2 Aquarius
3 Pisces
4 Aries
5 Taurus
6 Gemini
7 Cancer
8 Leo
9 Virgo
10 Libra
11 Scorpius
12 Sagittarius

▲ *Long before people even knew what a star was, they had divided them into constellations, or star groups. Very few of these patterns resemble what they are supposed to be. Leo, the Lion, is one of the few that do.*

▲ *During a year, the Sun appears to take a particular path through the celestial sphere. This path marks the center of the band of sky known as the Zodiac. There are 12 divisions of the Zodiac, each one represented by a constellation. The Sun seems to spend about one month in each constellation.*

▶ *This old star map shows the southern part of the celestial sphere. The dashed circle marks the path of the Sun, and the South Pole is shown a little way above the center. Unlike the north celestial pole, the South Pole does not have a bright star near it. At the foot of the map the celestial equator is marked, in line with Earth's equator.*

The Constellations

Most people think of a constellation as a group of stars. In fact a constellation is a definite area of the celestial sphere, with internationally-agreed boundaries. The areas fit together to make up the sky. The maps show major constellations of the sky. The faintest stars are those with the smallest dots; these should just be visible with the naked eye from well-lit cities. The outline of the Milky Way is shown, but this can be seen properly only under dark country skies.

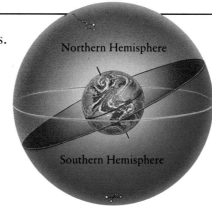

◄ Each map shows one complete celestial hemisphere, as seen by someone standing at the North or South Pole. The celestial equator is the dividing line between the two maps, and the Earth's axis points to the celestial poles, at the center of each.

CONSTELLATION FACTS

● In total, the sky contains 88 constellations. Most of these were named in ancient times. In A.D. 150 the Greek astronomer Ptolemy described 48 star patterns, including well-known ones such as Ursa Major (the Great Bear). Many of these had been recorded by Babylonian astronomers before 2000 B.C. Between the 16th and 18th centuries A.D., when explorers began venturing into the Southern Hemisphere, new parts of the celestial sphere came into view, and more constellations were added to the ancient ones.
● The largest constellation is Hydra (the Water Snake); the smallest constellation is Crux (the Cross).
● The faintest space object visible with the naked eye appears dimly in the Andromeda constellation. It is the Andromeda galaxy, 2.2 million light-years away.

▲ Ursa Minor (the Little Bear) is a constellation of the Northern Hemisphere. The bright star at the very tip of the bear's tail is the North Star, Polaris. Ursa Minor is visible from northern Europe and North America all year round.

NORTHERN HEMISPHERE

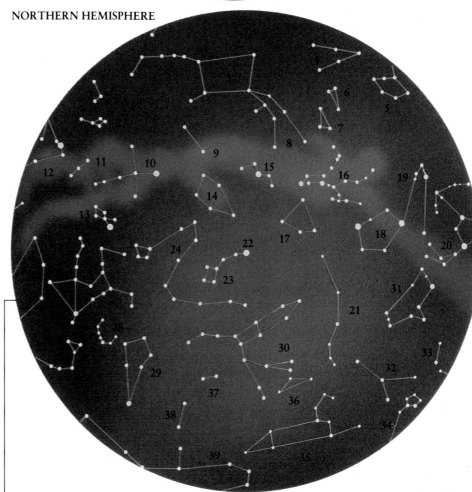

NORTHERN HEMISPHERE

1 *Equuleus* Little Horse
2 *Delphinus* Dolphin
3 *Pegasus* Pegasus
4 *Pisces* Fishes
5 *Cetus* Whale
6 *Aries* Ram
7 *Triangulum* Triangle
8 *Andromeda* Andromeda
9 *Lacerta* Lizard
10 *Cygnus* Swan
11 *Sagitta* Arrow
12 *Aquila* Eagle
13 *Lyra* Lyre
14 *Cepheus* Cepheus
15 *Cassiopeia* Cassiopeia

16 *Perseus* Perseus
17 *Camelopardus* Giraffe
18 *Auriga* Charioteer
19 *Taurus* Bull
20 *Orion* Orion (hunter)
21 *Lynx* Lynx
22 *Polaris* North Star
23 *Ursa Minor* Little Bear
24 *Draco* Dragon
25 *Hercules* Hercules
26 *Ophiuchus* Serpent Holder
27 *Serpens* Serpent
28 *Corona Borealis* Northern Crown
29 *Boötes* Herdsman
30 *Ursa Major* Great Bear

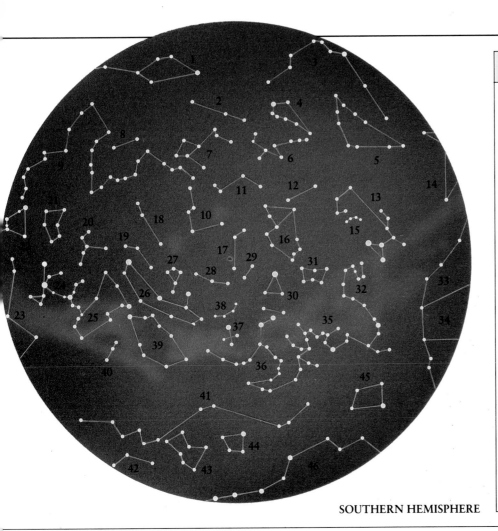

SOUTHERN HEMISPHERE

THE SOUTHERN CROSS

Australia

New Zealand

The constellation known as Crux, or the (Southern) Cross, appears on the flags of both Australia and New Zealand. The constellation contains five stars of different brightness. On Australia's flag the smallest star is shown with only five points, two less than the other stars. Only four stars appear on New Zealand's flag, all with the same number of points.

31 *Gemini* Twins
32 *Cancer* Crab
33 *Canis Minor* Little Dog
34 *Hydra* Water Monster
35 *Leo* Lion
36 *Leo Minor* Little Lion
37 *Canes Venatici* Hunting Dogs
38 *Coma Berenices* Berenice's Hair
39 *Virgo* Virgin

SOUTHERN HEMISPHERE
1 *Cetus* Whale
2 *Sculptor* Sculptor
3 *Aquarius* Water Bearer
4 *Piscis Austrinus* Southern Fish
5 *Capricornus* (Sea) Goat
6 *Grus* Crane
7 *Phoenix* Phoenix
8 *Fornax* Furnace
9 *Eridanus* Eridanus (a river)
10 *Hydrus* Water Snake
11 *Tucana* Toucan
12 *Indus* Indian
13 *Sagittarius* Archer
14 *Aquila* Eagle
15 *Corona Australis* Southern Crown
16 *Pavo* Peacock
17 *Octans* Octant

18 *Dorado* Swordfish
19 *Pictor* Painter
20 *Columba* Dove
21 *Lepus* Hare
22 *Orion* Orion (hunter)
23 *Monoceros* Unicorn
24 *Canis Major* Great Dog
25 *Puppis* Stern (of Argo)
26 *Carina* Keel (of Argo)
27 *Volans* Flying Fish
28 *Chamaeleon* Chameleon
29 *Apus* Bird of Paradise
30 *Triangulum Australe* Southern Triangle
31 *Ara* Altar
32 *Scorpius* Scorpion

33 *Serpens* Serpent
34 *Ophiuchus* Serpent Holder
35 *Lupus* Wolf
36 *Centaurus* Centaur
37 *Crux* (Southern) Cross
38 *Musca* Fly
39 *Vela* Sails (of Argo)
40 *Pyxis* Mariner's Compass
41 *Hydra* Water Monster
42 *Sextans* Sextant
43 *Crater* Cup
44 *Corvus* Crow
45 *Libra* Scales
46 *Virgo* Virgin

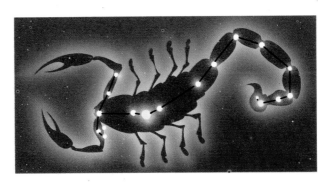

◀ *The constellation Scorpius (the Scorpion) can be seen in the Southern Hemisphere. The most prominent star in its body is Antares, a giant star about 500 light-years away. Antares is 10,000 times more luminous than our Sun.*

OBSERVING THE SKIES

The Birth of Astronomy

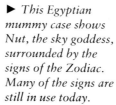

The people of early civilizations must have been aware of the fixed patterns of the stars in the sky, their repeated appearance and disappearance with the seasons, and the strange "wanderings" of the objects that we now call the planets. However, with no way of understanding their true nature, their astrological significance seemed the most important thing about them. The night sky was divided up into constellations, and they and the planets were given names. But right up until the beginning of the 17th century most people thought that the Earth was at the center of the universe.

Astronomical knowledge took a major leap forward in the early 17th century. The newly invented telescope was first turned to the sky, and Johannes Kepler proved that the planets move around the Sun, not the Earth. Modern astronomy was born.

ANCIENT ASTRONOMY

In ancient civilizations astronomy was closely linked to astrology, the belief that events in the sky can affect the lives of people on Earth. The positions of the planets were observed for astrological predictions. The duties of priests and astronomers overlapped. For example, the Babylonian ziggurat below was half-temple and half-observatory.

A ziggurat

▲ Astronomers in China were charting the positions of the stars as early as the 1300s B.C. The Big Dipper appears on this old star map.

► This Egyptian mummy case shows Nut, the sky goddess, surrounded by the signs of the Zodiac. Many of the signs are still in use today.

◄ Stonehenge, in England, dates from about 5,000 years ago. The Hele Stone (in the distance) seems to have been accurately placed to mark the position of midsummer sunrise. This event was important. In an age without calendars, the Sun's position as it rose and set was the simplest guide to the year's seasons.

VIEWS OF THE UNIVERSE

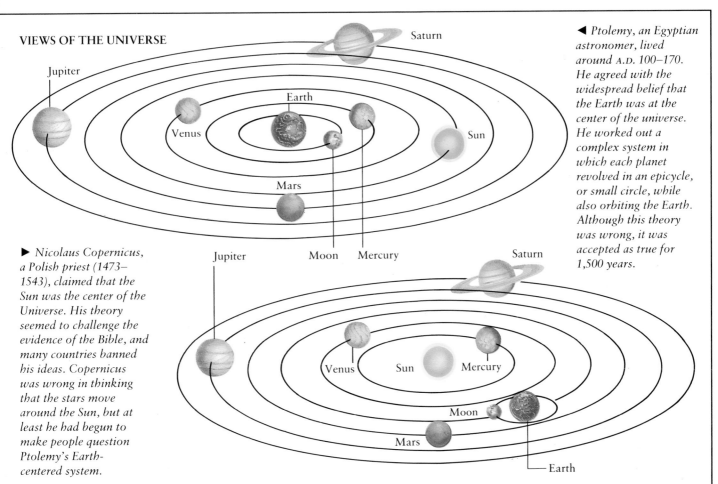

◄ *Ptolemy, an Egyptian astronomer, lived around A.D. 100–170. He agreed with the widespread belief that the Earth was at the center of the universe. He worked out a complex system in which each planet revolved in an epicycle, or small circle, while also orbiting the Earth. Although this theory was wrong, it was accepted as true for 1,500 years.*

► *Nicolaus Copernicus, a Polish priest (1473–1543), claimed that the Sun was the center of the Universe. His theory seemed to challenge the evidence of the Bible, and many countries banned his ideas. Copernicus was wrong in thinking that the stars move around the Sun, but at least he had begun to make people question Ptolemy's Earth-centered system.*

JOHANNES KEPLER

The German mathematician Johannes Kepler (1571–1630) analyzed naked-eye observations of the planet Mars to prove that the planets move around the Sun in elliptical orbits.

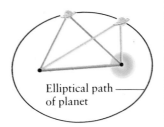

Elliptical path of planet

▼ *Kepler's Second Law states that an imaginary line between the Sun and a planet covers equal areas in equal times. This means that the planet moves faster when near the Sun.*

▲ *In an elliptical orbit there are two points, equally distant from the center. The Sun is at one point; there is nothing at the other. The farther apart the two points, the more elliptical the orbit.*

AREA A = AREA B

Distance traveled

Planet far from the Sun

Area A = x days

Sun

Area B = x days

Distance traveled

Imaginary line

Planet close to the Sun

DATE	EARLY EVENTS IN ASTRONOMY (Astronomer in parentheses)
3000 B.C.	Earliest Babylonian astronomical records.
2900	Construction of the stone circle begins at Stonehenge.
2137	Two Chinese astronomers beheaded for failing to predict a solar eclipse.
280	First suggestion that the Earth orbits the Sun (Aristarchus).
270	First accurate measurement of the size of the Earth (Eratosthenes).
130	First comprehensive naked-eye star catalog drawn up (Hipparchus).
A.D. 140	Theory put forward showing the Earth at the center of the universe (Ptolemy).
903	Accurate star positions measured with naked eye (Al-Sufi).
1054	Supernova seen in the constellation Taurus (Chinese observers).
1433	The most complete star catalog yet published (Ulugh Beigh).
1543	Theory published suggesting the Sun is the center of the Universe (Nicolaus Copernicus).
1572	Supernova visible in daylight in Cassiopeia (studied by Tycho Brahe).

Optical Astronomy

In dim light, the pupil of the human eye opens up to about 0.3 in. (7 mm) across. Even this tiny "light collector" is able to see the Andromeda galaxy, 2 million light-years away. A telescope is an artificial eye with a larger opening, or aperture, which collects more light than the human eye. Therefore it makes stars look brighter and can reveal fainter and more distant objects. In 1608 a new age of astronomy began when the first telescope was made by Dutchman Hans Lippershey.

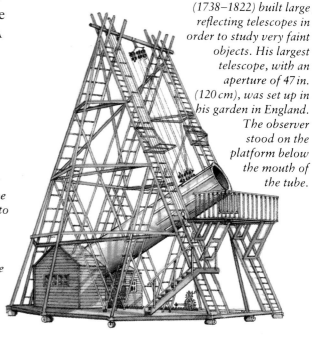

▼ *William Herschel (1738–1822) built large reflecting telescopes in order to study very faint objects. His largest telescope, with an aperture of 47 in. (120 cm), was set up in his garden in England. The observer stood on the platform below the mouth of the tube.*

GALILEO'S DISCOVERIES

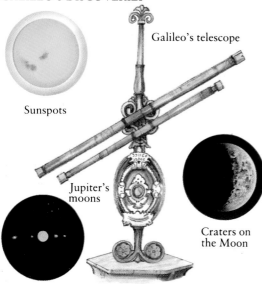

Sunspots

Galileo's telescope

Jupiter's moons

Craters on the Moon

▼ *Early refracting telescopes had to be very long in order to give a clear image. The telescope and observer had no protection from the weather. These fragile structures were called aerial telescopes.*

Galileo Galilei (1564–1642) was one of the first people to turn a telescope to the night sky. His first discovery was that the Moon was heavily cratered, instead of being perfectly smooth, as Ptolemy had thought. He also discovered four large moons in orbit around Jupiter, and he observed spots on the surface of the Sun.

KEY DISCOVERIES IN OPTICAL ASTRONOMY

▼ *Edwin Hubble used this 100-inch (2.4-meter) reflecting telescope to discover the expansion of the universe.*

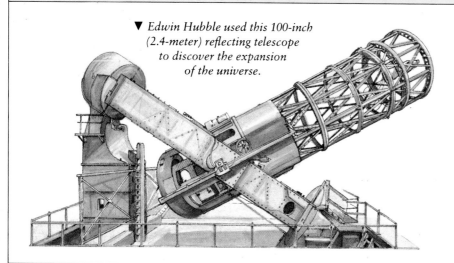

• In 1609 Galileo first turned a telescope to the sky; his observations of the phases of Venus confirmed Copernicus's theory that the Earth is not the center of the universe.
• The discovery of Uranus in 1781 extended our knowledge of the Solar System. Uranus was the first planet to be discovered by telescope.
• In 1838 telescopic observation meant that the distance to a star could be measured for the first time—by F. W. Bessel in Germany.
• In the 1920s Edwin Hubble used his observations at Mt. Wilson to show that the universe is expanding.

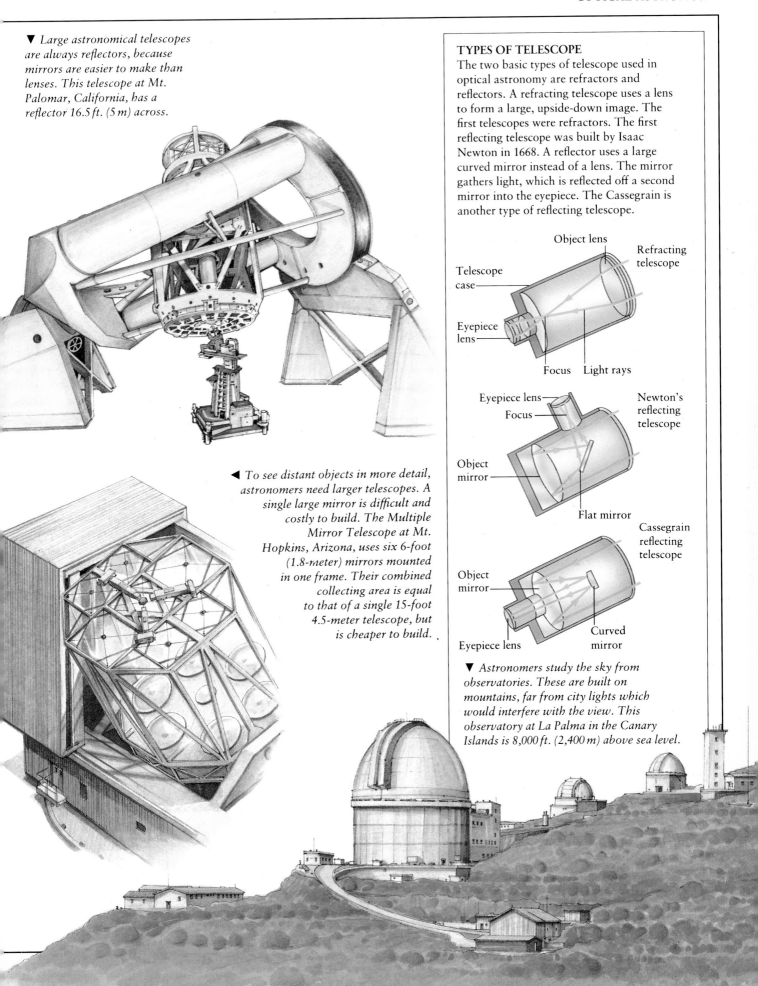

▼ *Large astronomical telescopes are always reflectors, because mirrors are easier to make than lenses. This telescope at Mt. Palomar, California, has a reflector 16.5 ft. (5 m) across.*

TYPES OF TELESCOPE

The two basic types of telescope used in optical astronomy are refractors and reflectors. A refracting telescope uses a lens to form a large, upside-down image. The first telescopes were refractors. The first reflecting telescope was built by Isaac Newton in 1668. A reflector uses a large curved mirror instead of a lens. The mirror gathers light, which is reflected off a second mirror into the eyepiece. The Cassegrain is another type of reflecting telescope.

Object lens

Refracting telescope

Telescope case

Eyepiece lens

Focus   Light rays

Eyepiece lens

Focus

Newton's reflecting telescope

Object mirror

Flat mirror

Cassegrain reflecting telescope

Object mirror

Eyepiece lens

Curved mirror

◄ *To see distant objects in more detail, astronomers need larger telescopes. A single large mirror is difficult and costly to build. The Multiple Mirror Telescope at Mt. Hopkins, Arizona, uses six 6-foot (1.8-meter) mirrors mounted in one frame. Their combined collecting area is equal to that of a single 15-foot 4.5-meter telescope, but is cheaper to build.*

▼ *Astronomers study the sky from observatories. These are built on mountains, far from city lights which would interfere with the view. This observatory at La Palma in the Canary Islands is 8,000 ft. (2,400 m) above sea level.*

Radio Telescopes

Besides sending out visible light, many astronomical objects emit radio waves, which are invisible. The Earth's atmosphere is completely penetrable to radio waves, which can pass through even the thickest clouds. For this reason, radio telescopes are very important in astronomy. Radio telescopes are a special kind of telescope that can collect radio waves and so "see" objects that are too dim or distant to be seen with ordinary telescopes. Quasars and pulsars were discovered by radio telescopes.

HOW A RADIO TELESCOPE WORKS

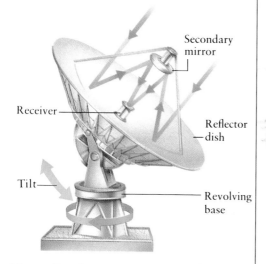

Secondary mirror

Receiver

Reflector dish

Tilt

Revolving base

Most radio telescopes use a concave dish to collect radio waves from space. The radio waves are reflected onto an antenna, which sends the signal to an amplifier to be strengthened. The signal will be processsed by a computer which can turn it into images. Radio waves have less energy than light waves, so radio telescopes must have a large dish to detect faint objects.

▲ *This unusual radio telescope at Nançay, France, has a fixed curved reflector. A second, movable reflector directs the radio waves from space onto the fixed reflector's surface.*

▶ *The main radio telescope at the Parkes Observatory, Australia, has a 210-foot (64-meter) dish. The largest "steerable" radio telescope in the world is at Effelsburg, Germany, and has a 330-foot (100-meter) dish.*

▶ *Only a little of the energy sent out by space objects passes completely through the Earth's atmosphere. This energy includes the visible light waves detectable by optical telescopes, as well as the shortwave radio waves picked up by radio telescopes. Some infrared radiation reaches the Earth's surface, but our atmosphere blocks most other forms of radiation from space.*

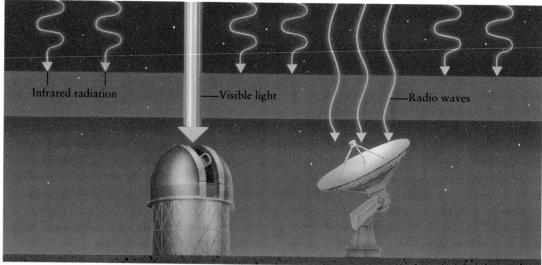

Infrared radiation

Visible light

Radio waves

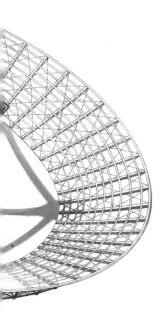

MAJOR RADIO OBSERVATORIES
• National Radio Astronomy Observatory, Socorro, New Mexico, includes the Very Large Array (VLA) *(below)*.
• Arecibo, Puerto Rico (1,000-foot dish, pointing directly upward).
• Green Bank, West Virginia (new 330-foot dish being installed by 1995).
• Australia Telescope, Culgoora, New South Wales (six 72-foot dishes, linked by computer to act like a much larger telescope).
• Effelsberg, Germany (330-foot dish).

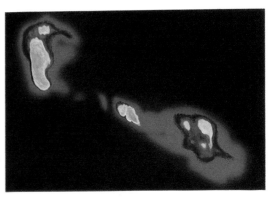

▲ *The clouds emitted by galaxy Centaurus A were recorded by the Very Large Array and turned into images by computer. They do not send out visible light.*

◄ *The VLA consists of 27 antennas, each 82 ft. across.*

► *Before 1900 no one had any idea how the Sun or other stars shone, and many people believed that the Milky Way was the most important galaxy in the universe, since no other galaxies had been identified. Some of the important astronomical advances made this century appear here.*

FURTHER FACTS

A radio telescope need not be a metal dish. The radio telescope that led to the discovery of the first pulsar was a collection of wires and poles, built in a field in Cambridge, England, in 1967. A simple metal bar may act as an antenna for radio waves.

DATE	KEY EVENT
1908	Ejnar Hertzsprung (Denmark) and Henry Russell (U.S.) discover that most stars belong to an orderly family, the "main sequence."
1912	Cepheid variable stars discovered by Henrietta Leavitt (U.S.). They are important, as their distance can be measured very accurately.
1915	Albert Einstein (Switzerland) publishes the *General Theory of Relativity*.
1923	Edwin Hubble (U.S.) observes Cepheids in the Andromeda Galaxy and measures the first distance between galaxies.
1929	Hubble proves that the galaxies are moving away from each other, and that the universe is expanding.
1930	Clyde Tombaugh (U.S.) discovers Pluto while searching for "Planet X."
1932	Karl Jansky first detects radio waves from space at Holmdel, New Jersey.
1937	First radio telescope dish built, measuring 31 ft. (9.4 m) across.
1958	The Earth's radiation belts discovered by James Van Allen's equipment on the American satellite *Explorer 1*.
1961	Quasar 3C 273 is the first to be discovered, by radio astronomers at Cambridge, England.
1965	Big Bang background radiation discovered by Arno Penzias and Robert Wilson at Holmdel, New Jersey.
1967	Pulsars discovered by Jocelyn Bell and Anthony Hewish at Cambridge, England.
1990	Light recorded from farthest-ever point to date.
1990	Hubble Space Telescope launched.

Space Telescopes

Putting a telescope into space, above the blocking, blurring effect of the Earth's atmosphere, sounds like an astronomer's dream. The Hubble Space Telescope (HST) is the latest and largest satellite designed to observe space objects. However, there are problems too. Carrying a telescope into space is an expensive and difficult business. If anything goes wrong while the telescope is in orbit there is no one to fix it, and its power supplies will eventually run down.

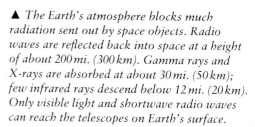

TELESCOPES IN SPACE

Some space observations are impossible from the Earth's surface because our atmosphere blocks out some types of radiation. X-rays and gamma rays from the Sun, red dwarfs, and exploding galaxies such as Centaurus A are blocked, as well as infrared rays from cool objects such as comets and nebulae. The atmospheric currents around Earth even affect visible light, making the stars twinkle. Images obtained in space are perfectly steady, and so more detail can be seen. An orbiting telescope can also observe the whole sky, which cannot be done from anywhere on the Earth's surface.

Centaurus A galaxy

Red dwarf

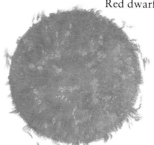

Comet

▲ The Earth's atmosphere blocks much radiation sent out by space objects. Radio waves are reflected back into space at a height of about 200 mi. (300 km). Gamma rays and X-rays are absorbed at about 30 mi. (50 km); few infrared rays descend below 12 mi. (20 km). Only visible light and shortwave radio waves can reach the telescopes on Earth's surface.

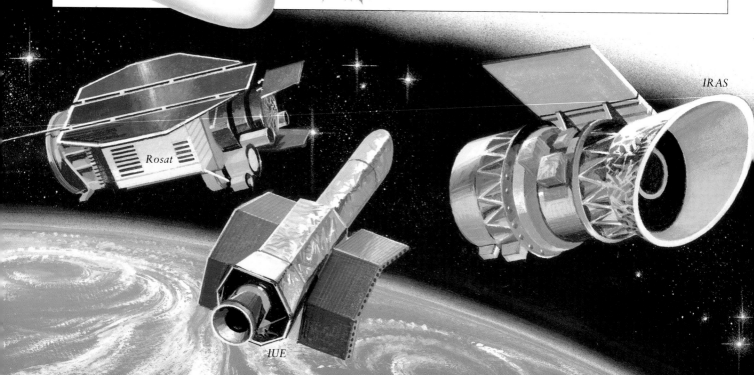

Rosat

IUE

IRAS

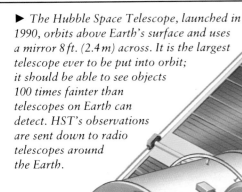

► *The Hubble Space Telescope, launched in 1990, orbits above Earth's surface and uses a mirror 8 ft. (2.4 m) across. It is the largest telescope ever to be put into orbit; it should be able to see objects 100 times fainter than telescopes on Earth can detect. HST's observations are sent down to radio telescopes around the Earth.*

Communication antenna

Door

Secondary mirror

Primary mirror

Communication antenna

Solar panel

◄ *The HST is really a giant video camera. In its "wide-field" setting it can produce images of complete star clusters and nebulae. In "faint-object" mode it can probe the space around a single star. It can also study the spectrum of a star or galaxy. Altogether there are five completely different ways in which the HST can be used.*

▼ *The HST has recorded an expanding cloud 50 times the diameter of the Solar System, surrounding a binary star, R Aquarii. Here, gas from a red giant is regularly detonated by its hot white dwarf companion. Material in the cloud is twisted by magnetic fields in space.*

▼ *Apart from the HST, other satellites orbit the Earth, sending back valuable information on space objects. Rosat, launched in 1990, is expected to record about 100,000 X-ray sources. These include dim stars, such as red dwarfs, which also give out some X-rays. The* International Ultraviolet Explorer *(IUE) was launched in 1978. The IUE studies ultraviolet light coming from stars. It is in a special orbit over the Atlantic Ocean so that its signals are received* directly by stations in Spain and the U.S. The Infra-Red Astronomy Satellite *(IRAS) was put into orbit in 1983. It discovered many young, invisible, cool stars, as well as several comets, including the comet IRAS-Araki-Alcock in 1983. The planned launch of the* Advanced X-ray Astrophysics Facility *satellite (AXAF) is in the late 1990s.*

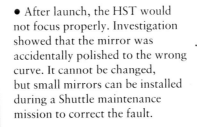

AXAF

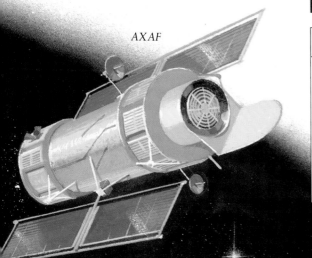

FACTS ABOUT THE SPACE TELESCOPE

● After launch, the HST would not focus properly. Investigation showed that the mirror was accidentally polished to the wrong curve. It cannot be changed, but small mirrors can be installed during a Shuttle maintenance mission to correct the fault.

● By computer-processing the originals to remove most of the blurred focus, some spectacular images have been obtained by the HST. However, this can be done only if the object is bright. Even then, the telescope is not showing as much detail as it should.

SPACE EXPLORATION

A Rocket to the Moon

Space travel was a fantastic dream for centuries. But to leave the Earth behind, it was necessary to build an engine powerful enough to travel at 6.8 mi./s (11 km/s), the speed needed to beat the pull of Earth's gravity. During this century, the invention of liquid-fuel rockets has made space exploration possible. Rockets are the only vehicles powerful enough to carry spacecraft away from the surface of the Earth. Since 1957, rockets have carried hundreds of satellites into orbit, where they can gather information about our universe. Rockets have launched space probes to other planets. Early Soviet rockets were powerful enough to launch cosmonauts (Soviet astronauts) into orbit, where they started building experimental space stations. And to fly astronauts to the Moon, U.S. space scientists constructed the three-stage *Saturn V*, the largest rocket ever built.

TO THE MOON AND BACK
(**1**) Rocket stages 1 and 2 launch craft into orbit and fall away. (**2**) Rocket orbits Earth then carries on to Moon. (**3**) Command and Service Module (CSM) turns around; locks with Lunar Module (LM). (**4**) Astronauts enter LM; LM separates from CSM. (**5**) LM lands; CSM orbits Moon. (**6**) Astronauts carry out tasks; LM blasts off and re-connects with CSM. (**7**) LM ditched. (**8**) Re-entry.

Earth

◀ *As the* Apollo *spacecraft approached Earth on its return from the Moon, small rockets were used to alter its course slightly. This ensured that the Command Module (CM) containing the three astronauts was on target for its fall toward Earth.*

LAUNCH TO SPLASHDOWN
The 360-foot (110-meter) rocket *Saturn V* launched *Apollo 11* to the Moon on July 16, 1969. On July 20, Buzz Aldrin and Neil Armstrong stood on the Moon's surface while the third crew member, Michael Collins, orbited in the Command Module (CM).

The CM was the only part of the spacecraft to return to Earth. Once it re-entered Earth's atmosphere its parachutes opened, slowing the CM down. Early U.S. missions would splashdown into the ocean, where the crew would be rescued by helicopters.

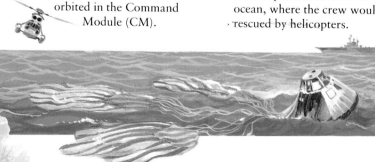

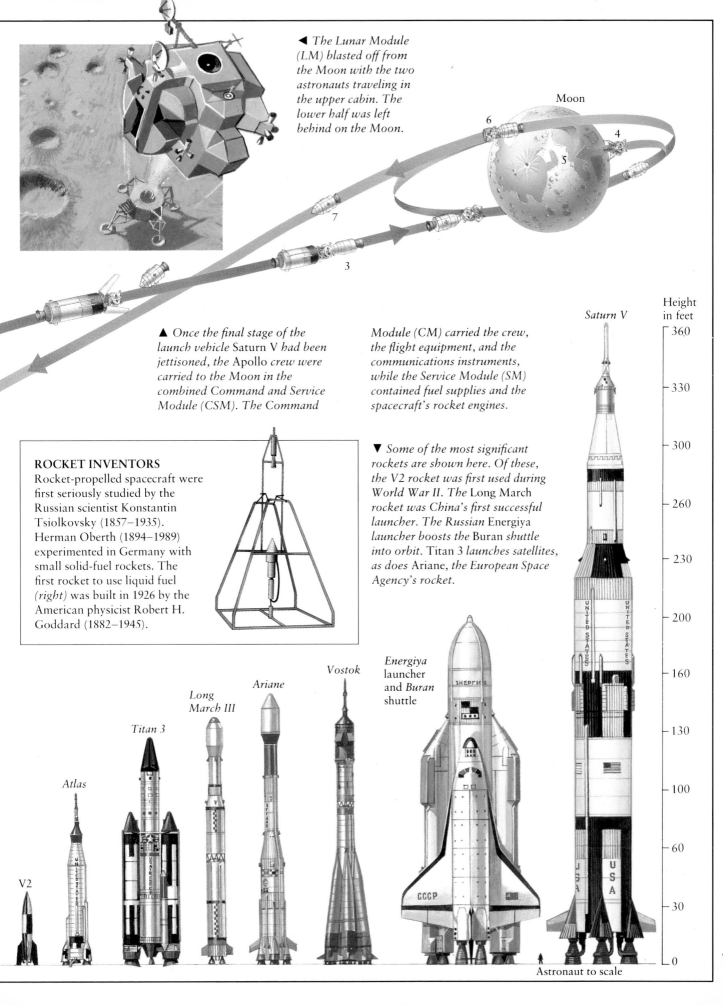

◀ *The Lunar Module (LM) blasted off from the Moon with the two astronauts traveling in the upper cabin. The lower half was left behind on the Moon.*

Moon

▲ *Once the final stage of the launch vehicle* Saturn V *had been jettisoned, the* Apollo *crew were carried to the Moon in the combined Command and Service Module (CSM). The Command Module (CM) carried the crew, the flight equipment, and the communications instruments, while the Service Module (SM) contained fuel supplies and the spacecraft's rocket engines.*

ROCKET INVENTORS
Rocket-propelled spacecraft were first seriously studied by the Russian scientist Konstantin Tsiolkovsky (1857–1935). Herman Oberth (1894–1989) experimented in Germany with small solid-fuel rockets. The first rocket to use liquid fuel *(right)* was built in 1926 by the American physicist Robert H. Goddard (1882–1945).

▼ *Some of the most significant rockets are shown here. Of these, the V2 rocket was first used during World War II. The* Long March *rocket was China's first successful launcher. The Russian* Energiya *launcher boosts the* Buran *shuttle into orbit.* Titan 3 *launches satellites, as does* Ariane, *the European Space Agency's rocket.*

Height in feet

Saturn V

V2
Atlas
Titan 3
Long March III
Ariane
Vostok
Energiya launcher and Buran shuttle

— 360
— 330
— 300
— 260
— 230
— 200
— 160
— 130
— 100
— 60
— 30
— 0

Astronaut to scale

73

Artificial Earth Satellites

An artificial satellite is a spacecraft placed in orbit around a planet. About 2,000 satellites have now been launched, for a number of purposes. Military satellites can spy, guide missiles, and even be weapons themselves. Communications satellites relay television, radio, and telephone transmissions. Weather satellites help with weather forecasting and also give immediate warning of cyclones. Scientific satellites may carry out studies of the Earth and its environment, or observe space objects.

▶ *Satellites are put into orbit aboard rockets or the Space Shuttle. The speed at which a satellite is launched has to be exactly right, or the satellite will fly off into space (1) or return to the ground (2). An orbiting satellite launched at the right speed will keep "falling" at the same rate as the Earth's surface curves beneath it (3), and so will never land.*

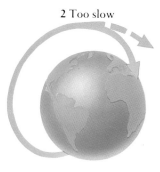

1 Too fast

2 Too slow

3 Right speed

Polar orbit

Geostationary orbit

Eccentric orbit

Circular orbit

◀ *Satellite orbits can pass right over both the poles so that all the Earth's surface can be surveyed. In a geostationary orbit, the satellite always faces the same part of the Earth. A circular orbit means that the satellite is always the same height above the surface of Earth, but if the satellite's orbit is eccentric this distance will keep changing.*

SPUTNIK
On October 4, 1957, the Soviet Union began the age of space exploration with the launch of *Sputnik 1*, the first artificial satellite. *Sputnik* orbited the Earth in 90 minutes and stayed aloft for 6 months.

▶ *Unless launched in the Space Shuttle, all satellites are carried in the upper stage of a launch rocket. When the rocket reaches orbit, the satellite is released. This means that discarded rocket parts continue to collect as extra, unwanted satellites above the Earth, and could one day cause a space accident.*

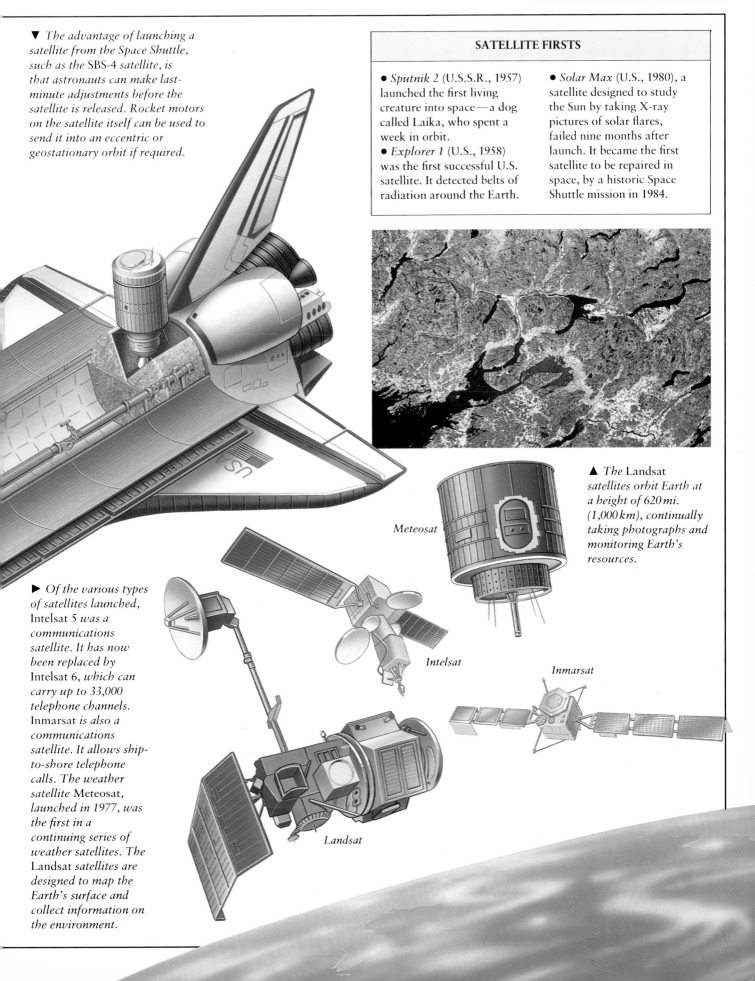

▼ *The advantage of launching a satellite from the Space Shuttle, such as the SBS-4 satellite, is that astronauts can make last-minute adjustments before the satellite is released. Rocket motors on the satellite itself can be used to send it into an eccentric or geostationary orbit if required.*

SATELLITE FIRSTS

● *Sputnik 2* (U.S.S.R., 1957) launched the first living creature into space—a dog called Laika, who spent a week in orbit.
● *Explorer 1* (U.S., 1958) was the first successful U.S. satellite. It detected belts of radiation around the Earth.

● *Solar Max* (U.S., 1980), a satellite designed to study the Sun by taking X-ray pictures of solar flares, failed nine months after launch. It became the first satellite to be repaired in space, by a historic Space Shuttle mission in 1984.

▲ *The* Landsat *satellites orbit Earth at a height of 620 mi. (1,000 km), continually taking photographs and monitoring Earth's resources.*

Meteosat

Intelsat

Inmarsat

Landsat

► *Of the various types of satellites launched,* Intelsat 5 *was a communications satellite. It has now been replaced by* Intelsat 6, *which can carry up to 33,000 telephone channels.* Inmarsat *is also a communications satellite. It allows ship-to-shore telephone calls. The weather satellite* Meteosat, *launched in 1977, was the first in a continuing series of weather satellites. The* Landsat *satellites are designed to map the Earth's surface and collect information on the environment.*

Space Probes

The first successful space probe was *Luna 2* (U.S.S.R.), which hit the Moon in 1959. Since then, probes have visited every planet in the Solar System apart from Pluto. These robot explorers have provided close-up pictures of worlds billions of miles away. The images are so clear that it is hard to appreciate the technical problems that were overcome. For example, the *Voyager 2* pictures from the edge of the Solar System were transmitted using the same voltage as two car batteries!

▼ *The first artificial object to reach another world was the Soviet probe* Luna 2, *which crashed into the Moon on September 13, 1959. Luna 1 had missed.*

▼ Luna 9 *was the first spacecraft to make a soft landing on the Moon, on February 3, 1966. It returned the first pictures of the Moon's surface.*

Luna 2

Luna 9

Mariner 10

◄ *Mariner 10 was the first probe to visit two planets. It flew past Venus and then Mercury in 1974.*

◄ *Pioneer-Venus 2 sent four probes into the atmosphere of Venus on December 9, 1978, while Pioneer-Venus 1 went into orbit.*

Mariner 2

THE FIRST VEHICLE ON THE MOON
The Lunokhods were unmanned Moon cars launched by the U.S.S.R. in 1970 and 1973. They were controlled from Earth by radio, and traveled the surface collecting data.

Pioneer-Venus 2

► *Mariner 2 was the first successful probe to visit a planet. It flew past Venus on December 14, 1962, and made temperature measurements.*

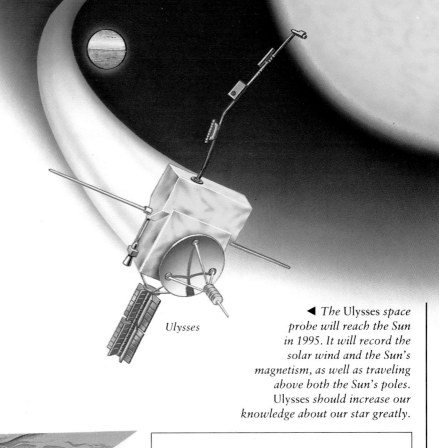

SLINGSHOT LAUNCH

To the Sun via Jupiter! Space probes can be speeded on their way, or have their course changed, by using the pull of another planet's gravity as a free energy source. The *Ulysses* probe, launched in 1990, used Jupiter's gravity to swing it into a vertical path that will pass above the Sun's poles.

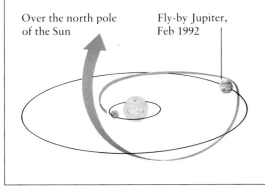

Over the north pole of the Sun

Fly-by Jupiter, Feb 1992

Ulysses

◄ *The* Ulysses *space probe will reach the Sun in 1995. It will record the solar wind and the Sun's magnetism, as well as traveling above both the Sun's poles.* Ulysses *should increase our knowledge about our star greatly.*

DEEP SPACE NETWORK

There is no second chance to receive data transmitted by a space probe, so there must always be a receiving station on Earth able to make contact. The Deep Space Network (DSN) has three main stations around the world so that all directions in the Solar System are covered.

Red

Blue

Green

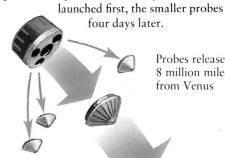

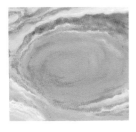

▲ *Color pictures were made from separate red, blue, and green images taken by* Voyager.

Deep Space Network, Australia

Deep Space Network, Spain

Deep Space Network, West Coast, U.S.

▲ *A telescope in Australia uses a 210-foot (64-meter) diameter antenna to receive signals.*

▲ *Eight hours later, the Spanish station near Madrid is facing the same direction in space.*

▲ *Commands to spacecraft are usually sent from the Goldstone station in California.*

PIONEER-VENUS 2

Pioneer-Venus 2 acted as a carrier to four smaller probes on the way to Venus in 1978. As it approached Venus, *Pioneer* launched its four probes toward different parts of the planet. The main probe was launched first, the smaller probes four days later.

Probes released 8 million miles from Venus

Large probe reaches atmosphere first

Parachute opens and aeroshell abandoned

Probe reaches surface 56 minutes after entering atmosphere

Life in Space

When an astronaut travels into space, the familiar background to life—day and night, gravity, natural air, sunshine, and exercise—is suddenly cut off. Astronauts undergo vigorous training to cope with the artificial space environment. Just to endure lift-off, which makes the body feel like it is being squashed, astronauts have to be extremely fit. As everything in the cabin is weightless, astronauts have to learn how to eat, sleep, move, and keep healthy in a world without gravity.

FACTS ABOUT PEOPLE IN SPACE

April 12, 1961: First man in space (Yuri Gagarin, U.S.S.R.).
June 16, 1963: First woman in space (Valentina Tereshkova, U.S.S.R.).
March 18, 1965: First spacewalk (Alexei Leonov, U.S.S.R.).

Valentina Tereshkova

U.S./U.S.S.R. link-up

Yuri Gagarin

December 1968: First manned flight around the Moon (*Apollo 8*, U.S.A.).
July 20, 1969: First Moon landing (*Apollo 11*, U.S.A.).
May 1973: First fully successful space station (*Skylab*, U.S.A.).
July 1975: First docking of U.S. and Soviet spacecraft (*Apollo 18* and *Soyuz 19*).
April 12, 1981: First Space Shuttle launched (*Columbia*, U.S.A.).
January 28, 1986: *Challenger* shuttle explodes, killing all seven people on board. Crew includes teacher Christa McAuliffe.

Challenger explosion

▼ *A spacesuit must provide a supply of oxygen, remove carbon dioxide and other waste products, maintain atmospheric pressure and keep the astronaut comfortably warm. The latest suits worn on Shuttle flights allow the astronauts to spend many hours outside the spacecraft. These are known as Extra Vehicular Activity (EVA) suits.*

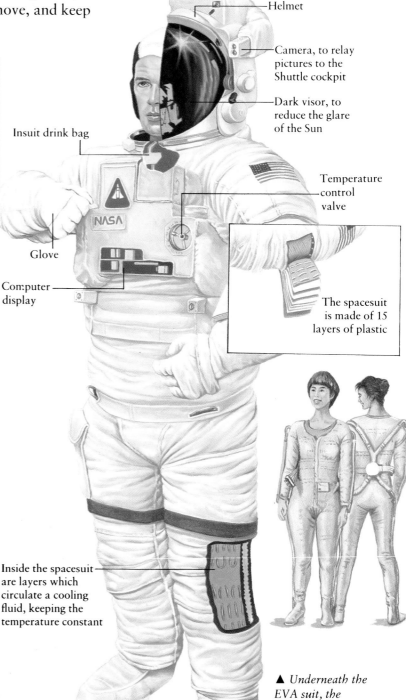

Helmet

Camera, to relay pictures to the Shuttle cockpit

Dark visor, to reduce the glare of the Sun

Insuit drink bag

Temperature control valve

Glove

Computer display

The spacesuit is made of 15 layers of plastic

Inside the spacesuit are layers which circulate a cooling fluid, keeping the temperature constant

Boots

▲ *Underneath the EVA suit, the astronaut's underwear helps to absorb sweat, which is one of the main problems with an airtight garment.*

▼ *There is no gravity in space, so liquid and food particles from an astronaut's dinner would float around the cabin. To prevent this, astronauts' food and drink are specially packaged.*

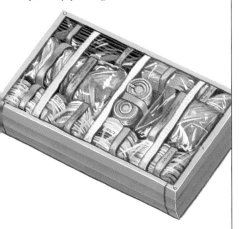

SPACE WALKING
When floating free in space, astronauts have nothing to push against to start themselves moving and no way of stopping either. The Manned Maneuvering Unit (MMU) used by U.S. astronauts contains small rocket thrusters pointing in different directions. When one is fired, the astronaut moves in the opposite direction. Lines tethering the astronaut to the spacecraft are no longer used with MMUs, as they could become dangerously tangled.

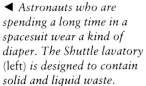

▼ *When sleeping, an astronaut is tied to the bunk or uses a secured sleeping suit. Sleep is timetabled, because there is no day or night in space.*

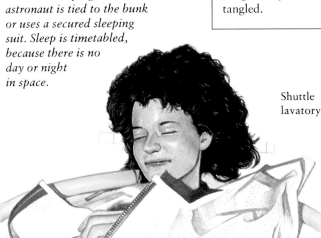

Shuttle lavatory

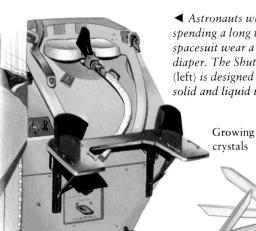

◄ *Astronauts who are spending a long time in a spacesuit wear a kind of diaper. The Shuttle lavatory (left) is designed to contain solid and liquid waste.*

Growing crystals

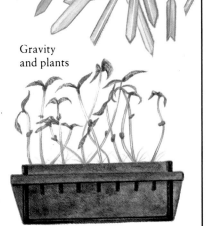

Gravity and plants

▲ *The health of astronauts is very important. The blood's circulation is affected by weightlessness, and this can cause sickness. Muscles may also start to deteriorate.*

► *Some Space Shuttle flights have carried a laboratory called Spacelab into orbit. Spacelab is used for experiments on the effects of weightlessness. Some of these experiments have been carried out on living things to discover how zero gravity affects them. Spacelab scientists have studied the growth of pine seedlings and the way a spider spins a web. Other experiments are related to industrial processes, such as the growth of crystals.*

Space Shuttles and Space Stations

The flight of the first Space Shuttle, *Columbia*, in 1981 heralded a new era in space exploration—the launch of reusable spacecraft. Before then, all spacecraft were used only once, making a space mission an expensive business. The Shuttle can take off like a rocket but land like a glider, and may be used many times. Soon Shuttle spacecraft will be involved with the ambitious *Freedom* project. This is planned to be the biggest-ever permanently occupied space station; it may be completed by A.D. 2000.

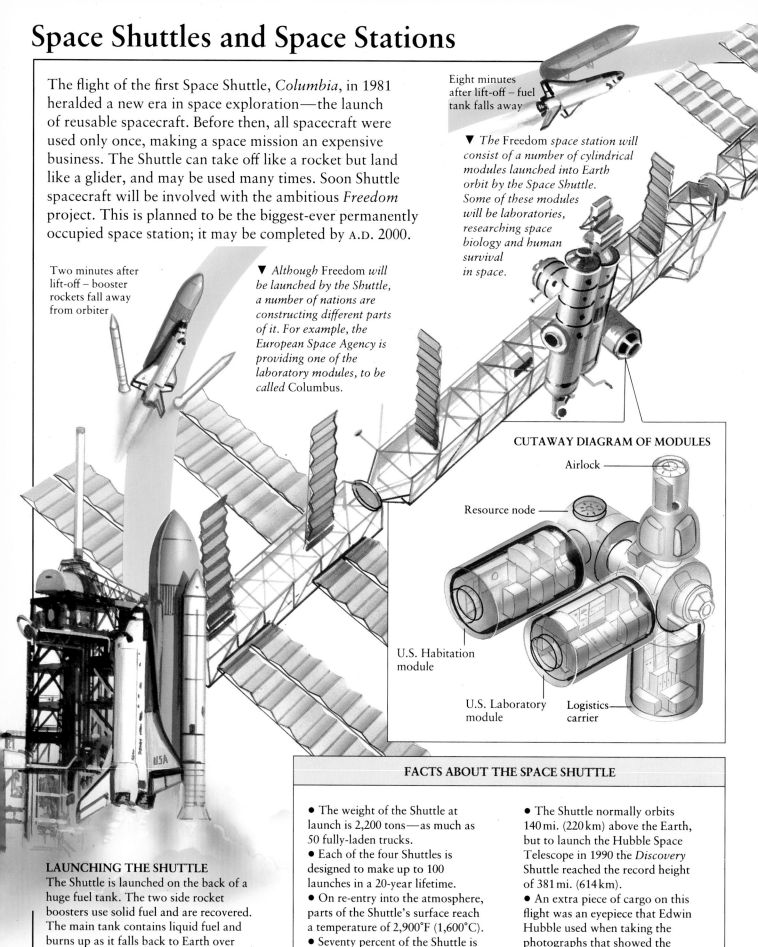

Eight minutes after lift-off – fuel tank falls away

▼ The Freedom *space station will consist of a number of cylindrical modules launched into Earth orbit by the Space Shuttle. Some of these modules will be laboratories, researching space biology and human survival in space.*

Two minutes after lift-off – booster rockets fall away from orbiter

▼ *Although* Freedom *will be launched by the Shuttle, a number of nations are constructing different parts of it. For example, the European Space Agency is providing one of the laboratory modules, to be called* Columbus.

CUTAWAY DIAGRAM OF MODULES

Airlock

Resource node

U.S. Habitation module

U.S. Laboratory module

Logistics carrier

LAUNCHING THE SHUTTLE
The Shuttle is launched on the back of a huge fuel tank. The two side rocket boosters use solid fuel and are recovered. The main tank contains liquid fuel and burns up as it falls back to Earth over the Indian Ocean. The Shuttle's own rockets take it into final orbit.

FACTS ABOUT THE SPACE SHUTTLE

● The weight of the Shuttle at launch is 2,200 tons—as much as 50 fully-laden trucks.
● Each of the four Shuttles is designed to make up to 100 launches in a 20-year lifetime.
● On re-entry into the atmosphere, parts of the Shuttle's surface reach a temperature of 2,900°F (1,600°C).
● Seventy percent of the Shuttle is covered with heat-resistant tiles.

● The Shuttle normally orbits 140 mi. (220 km) above the Earth, but to launch the Hubble Space Telescope in 1990 the *Discovery* Shuttle reached the record height of 381 mi. (614 km).
● An extra piece of cargo on this flight was an eyepiece that Edwin Hubble used when taking the photographs that showed the expansion of the Universe!

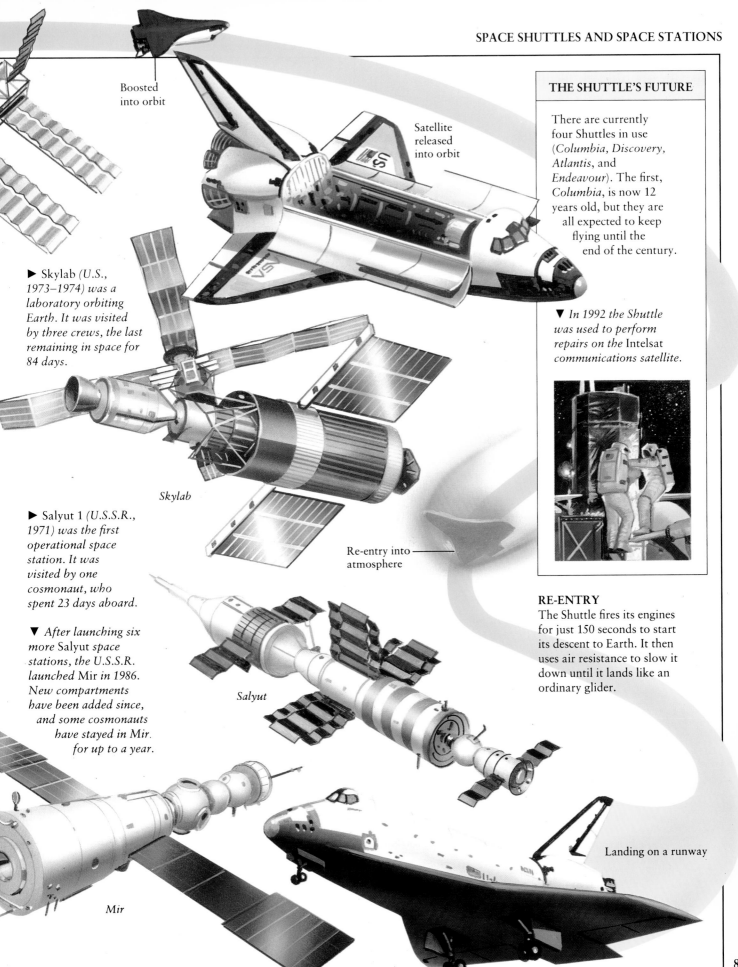

Boosted
into orbit

Satellite
released
into orbit

▶ Skylab *(U.S.,
1973–1974) was a
laboratory orbiting
Earth. It was visited
by three crews, the last
remaining in space for
84 days.*

Skylab

▶ Salyut 1 *(U.S.S.R.,
1971) was the first
operational space
station. It was
visited by one
cosmonaut, who
spent 23 days aboard.*

▼ *After launching six
more Salyut space
stations, the U.S.S.R.
launched Mir in 1986.
New compartments
have been added since,
and some cosmonauts
have stayed in Mir
for up to a year.*

Salyut

Re-entry into
atmosphere

Mir

Landing on a runway

THE SHUTTLE'S FUTURE

There are currently
four Shuttles in use
(*Columbia*, *Discovery*,
Atlantis, and
Endeavour). The first,
Columbia, is now 12
years old, but they are
all expected to keep
flying until the
end of the century.

▼ *In 1992 the Shuttle
was used to perform
repairs on the* Intelsat
communications satellite.

RE-ENTRY
The Shuttle fires its engines
for just 150 seconds to start
its descent to Earth. It then
uses air resistance to slow it
down until it lands like an
ordinary glider.

The Future in Space

The biggest problem facing the future of space exploration is not technology but cost. Because the Shuttle is still a very expensive craft to operate, several nations are working on a space plane which could take off and land using an ordinary airfield. Highly advanced jet engines would lift the space plane through the atmosphere, and a rocket would then carry it into orbit. Another cost-cutting project is the solar sail, which would use energy sent out by the Sun to "blow" spacecraft between the planets.

CODED MESSAGES

This message to possible other life forms was transmitted in radio code in 1974 toward a star cluster in the constellation Hercules. It will arrive in about the year 26,000.

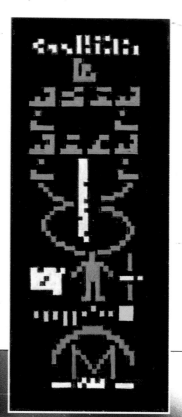

▼ *The solar wind of protons and electrons travels very fast, up to 560 mi./s (900 km/s), but has very little pressure. However, if large enough, a very light sail would gradually build up speed and could tow a load at spaceship velocity. A competition between three solar sails representing America, Asia, and Europe is due to be held in 1994. All three will be launched into space by the same rocket, and the winner will be the first to photograph the far side of the Moon. The illustration shows a possible design.*

◄ *Next century, there may be a permanent human settlement on the Moon. The building materials would be mined from the Moon itself. Radio telescopes would search the sky for signals from space, free from Earth's radio noise. The settlement would be an important research base for scientists.*

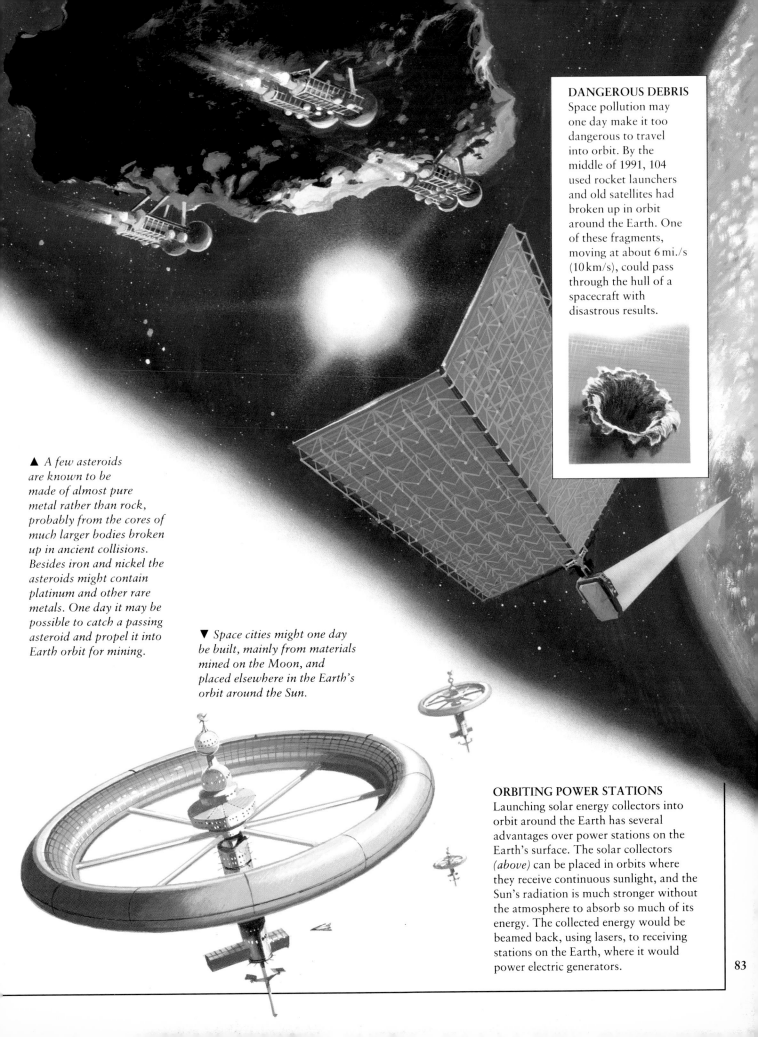

DANGEROUS DEBRIS
Space pollution may one day make it too dangerous to travel into orbit. By the middle of 1991, 104 used rocket launchers and old satellites had broken up in orbit around the Earth. One of these fragments, moving at about 6 mi./s (10 km/s), could pass through the hull of a spacecraft with disastrous results.

▲ *A few asteroids are known to be made of almost pure metal rather than rock, probably from the cores of much larger bodies broken up in ancient collisions. Besides iron and nickel the asteroids might contain platinum and other rare metals. One day it may be possible to catch a passing asteroid and propel it into Earth orbit for mining.*

▼ *Space cities might one day be built, mainly from materials mined on the Moon, and placed elsewhere in the Earth's orbit around the Sun.*

ORBITING POWER STATIONS
Launching solar energy collectors into orbit around the Earth has several advantages over power stations on the Earth's surface. The solar collectors (*above*) can be placed in orbits where they receive continuous sunlight, and the Sun's radiation is much stronger without the atmosphere to absorb so much of its energy. The collected energy would be beamed back, using lasers, to receiving stations on the Earth, where it would power electric generators.

GAZETTEER

Words in **bold** indicate an entry elsewhere in the Gazetteer or the Glossary.

Aldebaran: Red **giant star** that forms the eye of the **constellation** Taurus, the Bull. A hundred times as **luminous** as the **Sun**; 68 **light-years** away.

Andromeda galaxy: Nearest spiral **galaxy**, 2.2 million **light-years** away. May contain 400 billion stars. The Andromeda galaxy is the most distant object visible with the naked eye.

Antares: Red **supergiant star** that shines in the **constellation** of Scorpius. Wider than the Earth's **orbit** around the **Sun**; 500 **light-years** away and 10,000 times as **luminous** as the Sun.

Arcturus: Red giant and the brightest star found in the **constellation** of Boötes, the Herdsman. About 100 times as **luminous** as the **Sun**; 34 **light-years** away. Arcturus is the fourth-brightest star in the sky.

Ariel: Moon of **Uranus**, 720 mi. (1,158 km) across; orbits the planet in 2.52 days. Some of the craters on its surface are surrounded by white deposits, like those on our **Moon**. Ariel is crossed by smooth valleys.

Barnard's Star: Fourth-closest star to the **Sun**, a **red dwarf** six **light-years** away. Less than 0.001 percent as **luminous** as our Sun.

Betelgeuse: Red **supergiant star** that shines in Orion. Larger than the orbit of **Mars**, and about 40,000 times as **luminous** as our **Sun**; 330 **light-years** away. Betelgeuse may eventually turn into a **supernova**.

Callisto: Satellite of **Jupiter**, 2,980 mi. (4,800 km) across; orbits the planet in 16.7 days. Surface densely cratered.

Canopus: Giant **star** that shines in the **constellation** Carina, the Keel. Much hotter than the **Sun** and about 400 times as **luminous**; 74 **light-years** away. Second brightest star in the sky after **Sirius**.

Capella: Yellow giant star that shines in the **constellation** Auriga, the Charioteer. About the same temperature as the **Sun** but 100 times as **luminous**; 41 **light-years** away.

Centaurus A: Giant elliptical **galaxy**, 16 million **light-years** away. Seems to be erupting, sending out strong radio signals as well as X-rays. The nearest radio galaxy to our Solar System.

Ceres: The largest **asteroid** and the first to be discovered. About 600 mi. (1,000 km) across; it orbits the **Sun** every 4.6 Earth years.

Charon: Pluto's only known **satellite**, 745 mi. (1,200 km) across. The two bodies **orbit** each other at a distance of 11,900 mi. (19,130 km) in 6.38 days.

Chiron: Once thought to be an unusual **asteroid**, orbiting the **Sun** between Saturn and Uranus; now classed as a **comet**. A faint hazy **coma** is sometimes seen around it.

Crab Nebula: Expanding cloud from an exploding star (**supernova**) observed by Chinese astronomers in 1054. About 3,600 **light-years** away. Material from the supernova is flying outward at more than 600 mi./s (1,000 km/s). At the center of the Crab Nebula is the **pulsar** CM Tauri, which pulses 30 times a second.

Cygnus A: Galaxy, and the strongest source of radio waves in the entire sky. However, it is so far away that it appears as a dim speck even with the strongest telescopes.

Cygnus X-1: Powerful X-ray source. This radiation is believed to come from gas heated to 18 million °F (10 million °C) as it is dragged down onto a neutron star—or possibly into a black hole—from the other star in a binary system.

Deimos: Satellite of **Mars**, measuring about 7 mi. by 9 mi. (11 km by 15 km). Orbits Mars in 1.26 days.

Dione: Heavily cratered **satellite** of **Saturn**, 700 mi. (1,120 km) across; orbits Saturn in 2.7 days.

Earth: Third planet from the **Sun**, 7,926 mi. (12,756 km) across. Two-thirds of the surface is covered with liquid water. Only planet known to support life.

Enceladus: Satellite of **Saturn**, about 300 mi. (500 km) across; orbits the planet in 1.4 days. Has a smooth, icy surface with few craters.

Europa: Satellite of **Jupiter**, 1,950 mi. (3,138 km) across; takes 3.6 days to orbit the planet. It is made of ice.

Ganymede: Satellite of **Jupiter**, 3,270 mi. (5,262 km) across; orbits Jupiter in 7.2 days. Largest satellite in the **Solar System**. Ganymede is cratered, but unlike our **Moon** also shows signs that its crust has moved and folded, creating mountains and valleys.

Halley's Comet: Most famous of all **comets**, orbiting the **Sun** in 76 years on average. Last passed close to the Sun in 1985–1986 and will do so again in 2061.

Hyperion: Satellite of **Saturn**, irregular body about 185 mi. (300 km) across; orbits the planet in 21.3 days.

Iapetus: Satellite of **Saturn**, 930 mi. (1,500 km) across; takes 79 days to complete an orbit. One of its hemispheres is coal-black.

Io: Satellite of **Jupiter**, 2,256 mi. (3,630 km) across and orbiting in 1.8 days. Most active body in the **Solar System**—its surface is a waste of sulfur deposits and live volcanoes.

Jupiter: Largest planet in the **Solar System**. Its diameter is 88,730 mi. (142,800 km); its day lasts less than 10 hours. Has no solid surface and is made principally of hydrogen. Most famous surface feature is the cyclone known as the Great Red Spot.

Local Group: Cluster of more than 30 **galaxies**, including the **Milky Way** and the **Andromeda galaxy**. Extends over 5 million **light-years** of space.

Local Supercluster: "Cluster of clusters" of **galaxies**; includes the **Local Group**, also a much larger group known as the **Virgo Cluster**, and many other clusters and galaxies. About 100 million **light-years** across.

Magellanic Clouds: Two satellite galaxies of the **Milky Way**, dwarf irregulars less than 200,000 **light-years** away.

Mars: Fourth planet from the **Sun**; 4,217 mi. (6,787 km) across. Has little **atmosphere** and appears dead, but parts of its surface wrinkled and split open when it was young and hot. Features that look like dried-up river beds suggest water once ran on Mars.

Mercury: Innermost planet, only 2,780 mi. (4,880 km) across. Crater-covered, its rocks are oven-hot where they are exposed to the **Sun**.

Milky Way: Spiral **galaxy** containing at least 100 billion stars, including the **Sun**. Larger than many galaxies, but much smaller than some. Probably formed about 14 billion years ago.

Mimas: Satellite of **Saturn**, 243 mi. (392 km) across; orbits the planet in only 23 hours. One of the craters on Mimas's surface is a quarter of the satellite's own diameter.

Miranda: **Satellite** of **Uranus**, 300 mi. (480 km) across; orbits the planet in 1.4 days. Perhaps the most puzzling satellite in the **Solar System**, it looks as if it has been roughly put together using separate lumps of material.

Missing mass: Invisible matter believed to be present in the **universe** because of its **gravitational** effect. Amounts to approximately 10 times the mass of the **stars** and **nebulae** that are visible.

Moon: **Earth**'s satellite, 2,160 mi. (3,476 km) in diameter; orbits Earth in 27.3 days. Like most satellites it has a crater-covered surface. The smoother plains caused by lava flooding through the crust are not as common as on other satellites.

Neptune: Usually, the eighth planet from the Sun; 31,000 mi. (49,500 km) across. It has a surface of methane gas and winds of over 1,200 mi./h (2,000 km/h).

Nereid: **Satellite** of **Neptune**, about 190 mi. (300 km) across; takes 360 days to orbit the planet once, in a very eccentric orbit. Nereid was almost certainly a passing body captured by Neptune's **gravity**.

Oberon: **Satellite** of **Uranus**, 950 mi. (1,524 km) across; orbits in 13.5 days. Has an icy, cratered surface, but is also crossed by valleys several hundred miles long where the crust has split open.

Omega Centauri: One of over a hundred globular **star clusters** that surround the center of the **Milky Way galaxy**. Probably formed at the same time as the galaxy. Omega Centauri contains at least a million stars and lies about 17,000 **light-years** away.

Phobos: **Satellite** of **Mars**, only 17 mi. (27 km) long; orbits Mars in 8 hours.

Phoebe: **Satellite** of **Saturn**, 140 mi. (220 km) across; takes 550 days to orbit once, traveling around the planet in the opposite direction from most other bodies in the **Solar System**.

Planet X: Original name given to **Pluto** before it was discovered. Some astronomers believe that there may be another planet-size body in the outer **Solar System**, beyond Pluto's orbit.

Pleiades: Cluster of stars about 250 **light-years** away, often called the Seven Sisters. The stars were formed less than a hundred million years ago, making the cluster one of the youngest in the sky.

Pluto: Ninth **planet**, 1,370 mi. (2,200 km) across. Pluto takes 248 years to orbit the **Sun**. In 2113, at its farthest point from the Sun, it will be 4.6 billion mi. (7.4 billion km) away.

Polaris, the North Star: Yellow giant star, about 300 **light-years** away; 1,500 times as **luminous** as the Sun. To someone standing at the North Pole, Polaris would be overhead.

Proxima Centauri: Closest star to the Sun, 4.2 **light-years** away. A **red dwarf** about 10,000 times dimmer than the Sun. Belongs to a triple-star system which includes the bright **binary** Alpha Centauri, known as **Rigel** or Rigel Kent.

Quasar 3C 273: The first **quasar** to be discovered—a **galaxy** sending out as much energy as hundreds of ordinary galaxies. One of the nearest quasars to our Solar System.

Rhea: Crater-covered **satellite** of **Saturn**, 950 mi. (1,530 km) across; takes 4.5 days to orbit the planet.

Rigel: Brilliant **supergiant star**, 850 **light-years** away. About 40,000 times as **luminous** as the **Sun**; the seventh brightest star in the sky. Shines in the **constellation** Orion.

Saturn: Sixth planet from the **Sun**, with a diameter of 75,000 mi. (120,000 km), making it second to Jupiter in size. Saturn's bright rings are visible from Earth with a telescope.

Sirius: The brightest star in the sky, only 9 **light-years** away and about 25 times more **luminous** than the **Sun**. Has a dim **white dwarf** companion that was once much brighter than Sirius, but has already passed through the red giant stage.

SN 1987A: Bright **supernova** that erupted in the large **Magellanic Cloud** on February 24, 1987. Reached a peak brightness of about 50 million **Suns**.

Solar System: The **Sun**, its family of planets and their **satellites**, the **asteroids**, and **comets**.

Sun: Yellow **main sequence** star at the center of the **Solar System**, 900,000 mi. (1,392,000 km) across and about 4.6 billion years old. It is 8 "**light-minutes**" away from Earth.

Tethys: **Satellite** of **Saturn**, 660 mi. (1,060 km) across. Orbits the planet in 1.9 days. Shares its orbit with two other tiny moons, Telesto and Calypso.

Titan: **Satellite** of **Saturn**, 3,200 mi. (5,150 km) across; orbits Saturn in 15.9 days. Second-largest satellite in the **Solar System**. Has a methane **atmosphere** 120 mi. (200 km) deep.

Titania: Largest **satellite** of **Uranus**, 728 mi. (1,172 km) across; orbits the planet in 4.1 days. Titania is heavily cratered and has wide valleys, as though the hard surface split open in its youth.

Triton: **Satellite** of **Neptune**, 1,680 mi. (2,705 km) across; orbits the planet in 5.9 days, traveling backward like **Phoebe** in **Saturn**'s family. Spouts of nitrogen gas rising from its frigid, partly-cratered surface were observed by the *Voyager* space probe.

Umbriel: **Satellite** of **Uranus**, 728 mi. (1,172 km) across. Orbits the planet in 4.1 days. Has a very dark surface, covered with craters.

Uranus: The seventh planet, with a diameter of 31,700 mi. (51,000 km). Discovered with a telescope in 1781. The planet rotates tipped over on its side, instead of almost upright like all the other planets except **Pluto**.

Van Allen Belts: Two rings of atomic particles—protons and electrons—trapped by the **Earth's** magnetism around the equator. The inner belt is about 190 mi. (300 km) above the Earth's surface, the larger outer belt about 13,700 mi. (22,000 km) away.

Vega: **Main sequence** star, 26 **light-years** away. Shines in the **constellation** of Lyra. Vega is slightly more **luminous** than **Sirius**, but because it is farther away Sirius seems brighter in the night sky.

Venus: The second **planet**, Venus is 25 million mi. (41 million km) closer to the **Sun** than **Earth**. Heat has been trapped under the dense clouds that cover its surface, making it the hottest world in the **Solar System**.

Virgo Cluster: Large cluster of several hundred **galaxies**, about 50 million **light-years** away. Near its center is a giant elliptical **galaxy**, M87, which sends out strong X-rays.

1992 QB1: This body marks a new frontier of the **Solar System**. Orbit size is not accurately known, but its diameter is probably not more than 120 mi. (200 km). It will eventually be given a permanent name. Probably other bodies in this twilight zone are awaiting discovery.

GLOSSARY

Words in **bold** indicate an entry elsewhere in the Gazetteer or the Glossary.

Aerolite: Type of **meteorite,** made up of stony material; probably from the rocky crust of an ancient planetary body that broke up.

Airglow: Very dim glow that makes the night sky, even when seen from the darkest places on **Earth,** slightly brighter than the true blackness of space; caused by weak **aurorae.**

Albedo: The amount of sunlight a planet or **satellite** reflects back into space. The **Moon's** albedo is only 7 percent, because the rocks absorb the light. **Venus's** albedo is 80 percent because its atmosphere reflects light well.

Aphelion: Point on a planet's orbit at which it is farthest from the **Sun; Earth** is at aphelion around July 4th.

Apogee: Point on a **satellite's** orbit at which it is farthest from the planet.

Artificial satellite: Spacecraft put into orbit around a heavenly body.

Asteroid: One of countless thousands of small bodies orbiting the Sun; over 90 percent are found between the orbits of **Mars** and **Jupiter.** Most are less than a mile across, although the largest, **Ceres,** is about 600 mi. (1,000 km) across. Also known as minor planets.

Astronomical Unit (AU): Average distance of the **Earth** from the **Sun;** equal to 92,958,350 mi. (149,597,870 km).

Atmosphere: Layer of gas around a planet or star, held down by gravity. Small bodies with weak gravity, such as the **Moon,** have no atmosphere.

Atom: Smallest part or unit of an **element,** containing **protons, neutrons,** and **electrons.** Hydrogen is the simplest atom, with just one proton and one electron.

Aurora: Night-time display of colored lights which occurs when atomic particles pouring from the **Sun** strike gas **atoms** in the upper atmosphere and cause them to give out light.

Axis: Imaginary line through the center of a star or planet, around which it spins. The **Earth's** axis passes through the North and South **Poles.**

Big Bang: In theory, a huge explosion which saw the start of the **universe** about 15 billion years ago.

Binary star: Two stars in orbit around each other.

Black dwarf: The cold, dark corpse of an ordinary star, such as the **Sun,** after it has run out of fuel. Since they do not shine, no black dwarfs have yet been observed.

Black hole: Body with such strong **gravity** that nothing can escape, not even **light waves;** thought to be formed by the collapse of stars heavier than the **Sun.**

Brown dwarf: "Failed star," which did not get hot enough at the core for **nuclear reactions** to start, but is too large to be a planet.

Captured rotation: Movement of a **satellite** which keeps one half always facing inward as it orbits the parent planet; for example, our **Moon.** Such bodies used to spin quickly, but tides have raised a slight bulge on one side of the satellite, which has been slowed down and finally captured by the planet's **gravity.**

Celestial sphere: An imaginary hollow sphere with the **Earth** at its centre, on which the stars and planets seem to lie. As the Earth spins on its **axis,** the bodies seem to drift across the sky.

Cepheids: Important family of **variable stars.** These are **giant stars,** much more **luminous** than the **Sun,** which brighten and fade every few days as they swell and shrink.

Chromosphere: Lower part of the **Sun's atmosphere,** about 1,200 mi. (2,000 km) thick. Can be seen to shine deep pink during a total **eclipse.**

Coma: Hazy head of a **comet,** where gas and solid particles are escaping from the solid nucleus.

Comet: Body made of crumbling rock and ice, usually just a few miles across, which regularly passes near the **Sun** before swinging off into distant space. The Sun's heat may cause solid particles and gas to pour off in a long tail.

Conjunction: Moment that occurs when two astronomical bodies, one of them a planet or a moon, pass close by each other in the sky. The Star of Bethlehem may have been a conjunction of two bright planets.

Constellation: A group of stars found together in a definite area of the sky; 88 are recognized officially.

Corona: Outer atmosphere of the **Sun,** above the **chromosphere;** it extends several million miles into space.

Cosmology: The study of the universe, how it began and how it has evolved.

Crater: One of many scars on the surface of the rocky planets and almost all the **satellites,** produced by collisions with smaller bodies. Most formed at least 3 billion years ago. The **Earth's** craters have been smoothed out by weather and surface movements.

Dust: In astronomy, the minuscule grains of carbon that gather in vast clouds, or **nebulae,** many **light-years** across.

Dwarf star: Name given to most ordinary, or **main sequence,** stars. The Sun is a yellow dwarf. There are also **red, white,** and **black dwarfs.**

Eclipse: Occurs when the **Moon** passes into **Earth's** shadow (eclipse of the **Moon**), or when it passes in front of the **Sun** (eclipse of the **Sun**). Other bodies in the **Solar System,** and even **binary stars,** can eclipse each other.

Ecliptic: The path that the **Sun** seems to follow around the **celestial sphere** each year; in fact, it is the **Earth** that is moving around its orbit.

Electron: Subatomic particle with a negative electric charge.

Element: Substance containing just one kind of **atom;** common examples on **Earth** are oxygen and nitrogen.

Ellipse: The oval shape of the path followed by a planet, **satellite,** or **comet.** Ellipses may be almost perfect circles, like the **Earth's** orbit around the **Sun,** or very long and narrow, like the orbits of many comets.

Equation of Time: Difference between the correct local time and the time shown by the **Sun's** shadow on a sundial. In early November the **Sun** is 16 minutes "fast," while in the middle of February it is 14 minutes "slow."

Escape velocity: Speed at which a body needs to move if it is to escape completely from the gravity of a planet or **satellite:** 7 mi./s (11.2 km/s) for the **Earth** and 37.4 mi./s (60.2 km/s) for **Jupiter.**

Fireball: A very bright **meteor.** Some land on **Earth** as **meteorites.**

Galaxy: Vast collection of stars, **star clusters,** and **nebulae;** generally either spiral, elliptical, or irregular in shape. Dwarf galaxies may number just a few million stars—giant galaxies can contain a million, million stars.

Giant planets: In order from the **Sun: Jupiter, Saturn, Uranus,** and **Neptune.**

Giant stars: Old stars that have begun to expand and cool as they use up their hydrogen fuel. Red giants are the oldest, and have swollen up into a red mist. The **Sun** will eventually become a red giant. Blue giant stars have surface temperatures of 21,600°F (12,000°C)—much hotter than the Sun or a red giant star.

Globules: Protostars—dark clouds of **dust** and gas about one **light-year** across. Each globule is heating up at the center, and in a few thousand years will start to shine as a baby star.

Granulation: The mottled **photosphere** of the **Sun**, caused by gas breaking the surface and sinking back again.

Gravity: Force which attracts the bodies in the universe toward each other.

Infrared radiation: Sent out by cool stars and **nebulae**. Difficult to study from **Earth** and so satellites such as *IRAS* have been used instead. Infrared **wavelength** is longer than visible light but shorter than radio waves.

Ionosphere: Layer of **electrons** and **atoms** about 40 mi. (70 km) above the Earth's surface. Reflects certain radio waves, which can pass from one station on Earth to another by bouncing off the ionosphere.

Light wave: A beam of light consists of energy waves—about 2,000 in every millimeter. Red light has a longer wavelength than blue light. The waves contain packets of energy, called photons, and travel through empty space at a speed of 186,287 mi./s (299,792.5 km/s).

Light-year: Distance a wave of light will travel through empty space in a year—5,878,800,000,000 mi. (9,460,700,000,000 km). Used as a measure of distances in space.

Luminosity: Measure of how much light and heat a **star** gives out. Depends on its size and temperature. **Supergiant** stars are a million times more luminous than the Sun, but **red dwarfs** only a ten-thousandth of the Sun's luminosity are known to exist.

Lunation: The lunar month—the period from one New Moon to the next, lasting 29.5 days.

Magnetosphere: Stars and planets have their own magnetism. The magnetosphere is the surrounding space where atomic particles are trapped by this magnetism.

Magnitude: Apparent magnitude measures the brightness of a star as it appears in the sky. Absolute magnitude is the real brightness or luminosity of a star.

Main sequence: The family of normal stars, ranging from very bright and hot white stars, through cooler yellow stars like the **Sun**, down to the coolest dim **red dwarfs**.

Mass: Amount of material in a body. Different from weight (the force of **Earth**'s gravity pulling on a body).

Mesosphere: Belt of **atmosphere** lying between 30 mi. and 50 mi. (50 km and 80 km) above the Earth's surface.

Meteor: Streak of light left by a **meteoroid** as it burns up in the atmosphere.

Meteorite: Fallen **meteoroid**. Some are mainly stony (**aerolites**), others mainly nickel and iron (**siderites**).

Meteoroid: Body orbiting the Sun. They range in size from a grain of sand to extremely rare ones several yards across. They are seen only when they burn up in the atmosphere as a **meteor** or **fireball**. Large ones may land as a **meteorite**.

Midnight Sun: In summer, the part of the **Earth**'s surface near the pole is bathed in constant light and the **Sun** never sets, shining even at midnight.

Nebula: Cloud of **dust** and gas, usually many **light-years** across, in a **galaxy**. Stars are formed inside nebulae. Smaller nebulae can be thrown out into space when a **supernova** explodes.

Neutron: Atomic particle with no electric charge. Neutrons are found in the nucleus of every **element** except hydrogen.

Neutron star: Solid atomic matter remaining after the center of a **supergiant** star collapses in a **supernova** explosion.

Nova: Faint star which increases greatly in brightness almost overnight. Occurs in a **binary** system when gas passes from one star to another, causing an explosion.

Nucleus: Central part of an **atom**, containing **neutrons** and **protrons** (apart from hydrogen, which has no neutrons).

Occultation: Occurs when the **Moon** or a planet passes in front of a star, blocking it from view.

Opposition: A planet is at opposition when it lies opposite the **Sun** in the sky. This means that it rises above the horizon at sunset, and sinks below it at sunrise.

Orbit: Path traced out by a planet or **comet** around the Sun, or a **satellite** around a planet. Every orbit is an **ellipse**.

Ozone layer: Form of oxygen, high up in the atmosphere, which blocks out dangerous radiation from the **Sun**.

Parallax: If you move your head or body from side to side, a nearby object seems to move in front of more distant ones. This is parallax. The distance of nearby stars can be worked out by seeing how much they move in front of remote stars as the **Earth** follows its orbit around the Sun.

Penumbra: Partly-shaded ring around the dark center of a shadow, such as the shadow cast by the **Earth** on the **Moon** during a lunar **eclipse**. The lighter outer part of a **sunspot** is also called the penumbra.

Periastron: The smallest distance apart of two **stars** in a **binary** star system, as we see them orbiting each other.

Perigee: Point on a **satellite's** orbit where it is closest to the planet. In the case of the **Moon**, it is about 32,000 mi. (51,000 km) closer at perigee than at **apogee**.

Perihelion: Point on the elliptical orbit of a planet where it is closest to the **Sun**. The **Earth** is at perihelion around January 2.

Period: The length of time taken by a body to go once around its orbit.

Phase: The shape in which the sunlit part of the **Moon** or a planet appears in the sky. The **Moon, Mercury,** and **Venus** all change from a thin crescent to a complete circle.

Photosphere: Shining surface of the **Sun**. Its temperature is about 10,500°F (5,800°C).

Planet: Body orbiting a star and giving out no light of its own. May be mainly rock, like the **Earth**, or mainly frozen or liquid gas, like **Jupiter**.

Planetary nebula: Shell of gas thrown out by a star after a **nova** or **supernova** explosion.

Poles: The two points on a spinning body, such as a planet or star, where the **axis** passes through the surface.

Prominence: Eruption of hydrogen gas from the **Sun**'s surface.

Proper motion: The very slow change of position of the stars in the sky as thousands of years pass.

Proton: Atomic particle with a positive electric charge. Protons and **neutrons** form the nucleus of an **atom**, and the number of protons always equals the number of **electrons**.

Pulsar: Neutron star sending out a beam of light and radio waves as it spins. Each time this beam sweeps across the **Earth** we receive a pulse of **radiation**.

Quasar: Object producing as much energy as a hundred ordinary **galaxies**. Quasars are too far away from **Earth** to observe clearly, but seem to be galaxies with a special powerhouse at the center.

Radiation: Energy, and the way it passes through space, in pulses radiating outward like ripples across a pond. X-rays, light waves, and radio waves are different forms of radiation, with different wavelengths.

Red dwarf: Main sequence star with less **mass** than the **Sun**. Its surface temperature is only about 5,000°F (3,000°C), and it is less than a thousandth as **luminous** as the Sun.

Red shift: Because the universe is expanding, the **galaxies** are flying away from us. This spreads the light waves from the galaxies farther apart, making them seem redder.

Retrograde motion: The planets appear to move slowly in front of the stars, from west to east. However, when they are near **opposition** the **Earth's** speed makes them seem to move backward, or "retrograde."

Rings: Belts of solid particles—small rocky bodies, ice, and dust—orbiting the four **giant planets**. The particles may have come from a **satellite** that broke up in orbit.

Saros: Period of 18 years, 10 days, and 8 hours. Ancient astronomers found that **eclipses** of the **Sun** and **Moon** repeat after this interval.

Satellite: Body orbiting a planet. So far, 60 natural satellites have been found in the Solar System. Also known as a moon. *See also* **artificial satellite**.

Scintillation: *see* **twinkling**.

Seasons: Change from summer to winter; occurs because each of the **Earth's** poles turns toward and then away from the **Sun** during the course of the year.

Sidereal day: Time the **Earth** takes to rotate on its **axis**—23 hours, 56 minutes, and 4 seconds; measured by the stars rather than the **Sun**.

Siderite: Meteorite, consisting mainly of metal. Probably came from the iron-nickel core of an ancient planetary body that broke up.

Solar day: Time the **Earth** takes to rotate on its axis, measured by the **Sun**; exactly 24 hours long.

Solar wind: Steady outward blast of atomic particles from the **Sun**, reaching to the farthest part of the **Solar System**.

Spectral type: A way of classifying stars into groups according to the nature of their **spectrum**.

Spectrum: Color range produced when light passes through a prism. Different **elements** produce their own pattern of bright or dark lines in a spectrum.

Star: Ball of hot gas which gives out heat and light as a result of atomic reactions deep inside it.

Star cluster: Group of stars which formed from the same **nebula**. Open clusters are usually young and contain a few hundred stars of many different kinds. Globular clusters contain many thousands of old **red giant** stars, packed much more closely together.

Steady state: Theory put forward about 50 years ago, stating that the **universe** has always existed. It has been given up because the **Big Bang** theory is far better at explaining the discoveries of astronomers.

Stratosphere: Belt of **atmosphere** lying between 6 and 30 mi. (10 and 50 km) above the **Earth's** surface.

Sunspot: Region of the **photosphere** 900°F (500°C) cooler than its surroundings.

Sunspot cycle: Period of time, about every 11 years, when **sunspots**, flares and **aurorae** become more common. The next period of maximum activity will occur around the year 2001.

Supergiant: Rare type of star, several times as massive as the Sun and up to a million times as **luminous**. A supergiant will probably end its life as a **supernova**.

Supernova: Complete destruction of a **supergiant** star in an explosion as bright as a whole **galaxy**. A **neutron star**, or even a **black hole**, may be all that is left.

Terrestrial planets: The inner planets: **Mercury, Venus, Earth,** and **Mars**.

Tides: The gravity of two nearby space bodies makes them pull at each other's surface, producing tides.

Transit: Occurs when a **satellite** passes in front of a planet. **Mercury** and **Venus** sometimes transit the **Sun**, appearing as round black spots against the **photosphere**.

Troposphere: Lower layer of the **Earth's** atmosphere; about 6 mi. (10 km) high at the poles, and 10 mi. (16 km) at Equator.

Twinkling: Caused by heat currents in the **atmosphere** passing in front of the stars. The telescopic image dances, and fine detail is blurred. Large telescopes are usually built at a high altitude, where twinkling is less severe. Also known as scintillation.

Ultraviolet light: Invisible **radiation** sent out by the **Sun** and other stars. Most of it is blocked by the **Earth's atmosphere**, especially the **ozone layer**. Its wavelength is shorter than visible light, but longer than X-rays.

Umbra: Dark central part of a shadow, surrounded by the **penumbra**. The darkest part of a **sunspot** is also called the umbra.

Universe: All of space and everything that exists in it. The universe is infinite—it has no end. *See also* **Big Bang, Steady state**.

Variable stars: Stars that change in brightness. Eclipsing variables are **binary stars** where one star regularly blocks the light from the other one. Intrinsic variables are single stars whose **luminosity** changes.

Wavelength: The distance between waves of **radiation**. Examples are: long wave radio with waves of up to several thousand meters; heat radiation, waves of about 1 mm; visible light, about 2,000 waves/mm; X-rays, about 10,000,000 waves/mm.

White dwarf: Remains of a star, after it has become a **red giant**. Its surface is very hot, but because it has shrunk so small it is less than a hundredth as bright as the **Sun**.

Zodiac: A band of sky 20° wide with the **ecliptic** passing along the center. The **Moon** and all the **planets** (except **Pluto**) always lie within it. The Zodiac passes through the 12 Zodiacal **constellations**.

INDEX

Page numbers in *italic* type refer to illustrations.

Page numbers in **bold** type refer to key topics.

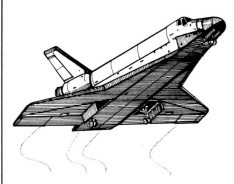
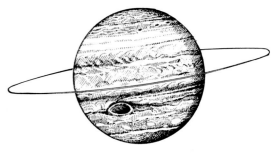

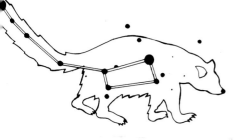

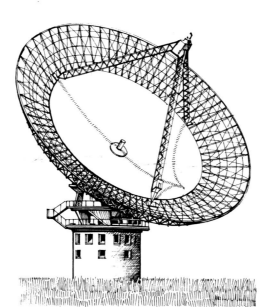

The publishers would like to thank the following artists
for contributing to the book:

Jonathan Adams 66–67, 69; Marion Appleton 22, 23, 36, 64; Peter Bull 80;
Joanne Cowne 27, 43; Richard Draper 14–15, 68, 69; Mark Franklin 62–63, 67;
Lee Gibbons (Wild Life Art Agency) 18, 19, 20, 22, 34, 36, 38; Jeremy Gower 49;
Ray Grinaway 80, 81; Terry Hadler (Bernard Thornton Artists) 78–79; J. Haysom 66;
Ron Jobson (Cathy Jakeman Illustration) 10–11, 12, 60;
Mainline Design 13, 15, 16–17, 20, 29, 35, 37, 41, 42, 43, 45, 46–47, 48, 49, 50–51, 60, 61,
62, 63, 65, 68, 72, 73;
Maltings Partnership 20, 21, 22, 24, 25, 26, 27, 30, 32, 34, 35, 36, 38, 40, 54–55,
58–59, 69, 70, 77;
Janos Marffy (Cathy Jakeman Illustration) 18, 32, 33, 56–57;
Josephine Martin (Garden Studios) 15, 31;
Michael Roffe 20–21, 23, 24–25, 33, 35, 36, 37, 39, 41, 42, 44, 52–53, 70, 71, 72,
73, 76, 77, 82–83;
David Russell 71, 74–75, 76, 77; Nick Shewring (Garden Studios) 57, 60;
Roger Stewart 13, 18, 20, 24, 28, 30, 36, 38, 40
and thanks to Mullard Radio Astronomy Observatory

The publishers wish to thank the following for supplying
photographs for this book:

Page 8 ZEFA; 11 Science Photo Library; 21 JPL/NASA;
23 Science Photo Library; 26 Science Photo Library; 27 ZEFA;
29 NASA; 31 NASA; 35 JPL/NASA; 37 JPL/NASA; 39 NASA; 40 NASA;
43 Science Photo Library; 44 Science Photo Library (top);
ESA (bottom); 47 NASA (top); Anglo-Australian Observatory
(centre right and bottom); 49 Anglo-Australian Observatory;
51 Science Photo Library; 54 Anglo-Australian Observatory;
58 Anglo-Australian Observatory; 59 Science Photo Library;
61 Royal Astronomical Society; 71 NASA;
75 Science Photo Library; 79 NASA

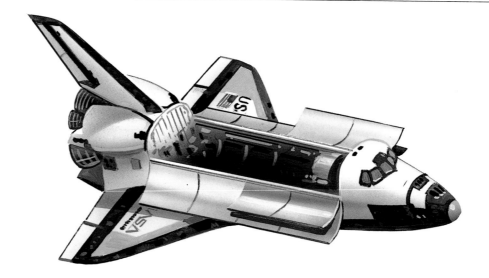